Empath Survival Guide:

A Beginner's Guide to Protect Yourself from Energy Vampires: Understand Your Gift and Master Your Intuition. Learn How Highly Sensitive People Control Emotions and Overcome Fears.

© Copyright 2019 by Jane Cooper

All Rights Reserved

Table of Contents

Introduction

Congratulations on purchasing *Empath Survival Guide and* thank you for doing so. Empathy is a word that is often used, yet many people miss the definition of the word. I will walk you through empathy, being an empath, and how to deal with energy vampires. The world needs more empathy, and this book is the first step you can take to understand the importance of empathy. And if you are an empath, you would know how to utilize your gift for the betterment of the world. The information you find in this book can be put to practice as soon as one wants to.

Matters of the heart are also challenging for empaths. There are those who, when they see a natural giver, they approach these empaths with the sole purpose of receiving, without intending to give anything. You will feel that the relationship is not right, yet you'll feel guilty about leaving. You'll be afraid of offending the other person. Before you know it, you'll be a sacrificial lamb stuck in a relationship that is doing nothing for you. Here, we outline ways to keep that from happening and to ensure that you receive as much in a relationship than you give.

We also delve into the issue of mental health. As an empath, you're highly vulnerable to mental health issues. Dealing with a mishmash of emotions every single day is no easy task. You have to be deliberate about self-care. To begin with, learn as much as you can about your personality. Going through this book is a good place to start. Self-awareness helps you recognize what is happening to you, and why you react the way you do. You then learn to anticipate certain reactions, so that you're not overwhelmed.

If you discover that your empathy level is high or advanced, you will also find many tools, practices, and guides here to help you manage intense emotions and maintain your energy reserves, shielding your essence from psychic vampires and toxic relationship dynamics. From the realms of western medicine, neuroscience, psychology, and metaphysical healing traditions, you will learn strategies for managing empathic power that can be combined and tailored to suit your individual needs. You'll be steered first towards the goal of finding joy and gratitude for your empathy, though it can indeed be challenging to manage. Secondly, your goal will be to find inner peace, a form of energetic balance that provides enough stability for you to weather whatever emotional storms life might throw at you.

The following chapters will discuss more empathic nature, the many gifts that empaths possess, the possible effects of empathy in the society, the relationship between empaths and narcissists, narcissistic abuse and how to avoid it. It will also focus on the best strategies that empaths should have to defend themselves from being manipulated, and the grounding for empaths. You will get to know why you need time alone as an empath and the best strategies you can apply when restricting yourself from going back to a narcissistic relationship.

There are many books on this subject on the market, thanks again for choosing this guidebook! Every effort was made to ensure it contains as much valuable information as possible. I am sure you will enjoy it!

Chapter 1: The Science of Empathy: (the Mirror Neuron System)

The words "empath" and "empathy" both stem from the Ancient Greek term "Empatheia," which is a hybrid of the words "en" meaning "in" or "at" and "pathos" which means "passion" or "feeling" but can also be interpreted to mean "suffering." This is etymological root is perfectly illustrative of empathy as a double-edged sword. Humans crave deep interpersonal connection and often find joy in shared passions, but when we open ourselves up to the blessings of those around us, we also open ourselves up to their sorrows, fears, and furies.

Within the past few decades, the fields of psychology, neuroscience, and many others have made enormous strides in research towards understanding the minds of those who do not display the "normal" amount of empathy. There are some conditions, such as autism or Asperger's syndrome, wherein a person seems able to detect the emotional energies of those around them, but simply lacks the necessary cognitive tools to interpret them or determine an appropriate reaction. These people often feel attacked or overwhelmed when the emotions of others resonate within them—which is a form of empathic sensitivity—but they often react by shutting down or self-isolating rather than trying to find a way to harmonious coexistence. It is not a struggle for these people to put their own needs first in interpersonal connections, even if it is at the expense of other people's feelings, but this isn't a malicious sentiment; it is primarily a self-preservation instinct in hyperdrive.

Alternatively, there are empathy-deficient personality disorders, such as narcissism, sociopathy, and psychopathy, wherein a person is capable of recognizing the emotions of others but feels personally detached from them. This is why we often describe psychopathic criminals as "cold" or "calculating." It is unsettling to imagine that a person could decide to take action, knowing that their behavior will cause pain or suffering in others and that they might remain unbothered by that fact or actually derive pleasure from it--but that is the thought process of an empathy-disordered individual. The feelings of others are considered unimportant because they do not impact their personal emotional sensations.

The general population holds a lot of misconceptions about people with these personality disorders, which are most evident within the criminal justice system. Many of us convince ourselves, for instance, that these people commit crimes of passion, temporarily losing their sense of right and wrong in the blinding heat of rage, or alternatively, that they are so mentally skewed as to be incapable of understanding how much pain and suffering they are causing. Unfortunately, neither of these possibilities proves true for these individuals. They do understand the impact of their actions and are capable of determining right from wrong, yet they choose to ignore these factors, hurting other people to serve strategic needs or for the sake of personal gain. In fact, people with these personality disorders generally display impressive skill with cognitive empathy, which you might think of as theoretical empathy; this allows them to theorize or predict the emotional reactions of others and makes them masterful manipulators.

When discussing those who struggle to display or feel empathy, it's important to remember that empathic abilities are fluid, not fixed in stone. Anyone who is willing to put in the effort can improve their empathic capabilities, even those who have been diagnosed with an empathy deficient condition or disorder. Physical empathy is often accessible to those who do not display emotional empathy, which may be a function of evolutionary development. Humans can better protect their physical bodies by recognizing physical pain in others and are biologically driven to mimic pleasurable behaviors (whether that means eating good food or enjoying sexual stimulation) by watching others and empathizing with their enjoyment of such activities. Since this form of empathy is often observable in scans of empathy-disordered brains, we must embrace the notion that empathy exists as a complex and fluid and scale. It is not like a light switch that is either flipped on or off.

Empathy is important because it allows you to simulate the cognitive and affective mental conditions of other people.

Neurobiological research studies have proved that empathy is a sophisticated encounter or phenomenon that can be explained in detail using a model consisting of top-down and bottom-up processing.

Top-down processing is also called the theory of mind or cognitive perspective-taking. This is a phenomenon where you fully imagine and understand the feelings of other people. It is centered on inhibition and control mechanisms. Available evidence shows that empathic brain responses are usually affected by distinct modulating factors.

I hope you are still with me! Researchers have come up with a new model that provides an explanation of the origins of empathy and other things such as contagious yawning and emotional contagion. The model demonstrates that the origin of a wide range of empathetic responses can be found in cognitive simulation. The model shifts attention from a top-down approach that starts with cooperation to one that begins with one cognitive mechanism.

According to a post-doctoral researcher in Max Planck Institute called Fabrizio Mafessoni, standard models of the origin of empathy concentrate on situations in which cooperation or coordination are the favorites. Michael Lachmann, a theoretical biologist, together with his co-author, looked at the possibilities that cognitive processes have a wide underlying range of empathetic responses including contagious yawning, emotional contagion, and other feelings such as echopraxia and echolalia. Echolalia is a compulsive repetition of other people's speech, while echopraxia is the compulsive repetition of other people's movements. Echolalia and echopraxia can evolve in the absence of mechanisms that directly favor coordination and cooperation or kin selection.

Lachmann and Mafessoni asserted that human beings and animals could participate in the act of stimulating the minds of other people or animals. You cannot read other people's minds because they are like black boxes to you. But as Lachmann put across, all agents have the same black boxes with members of their species, and they constantly run simulations of what other minds may be doing. This ongoing process or as-actor simulation is not always focused on cooperation. It is something that animals and human beings do as a result of a sudden impulse or in other words without premeditation.

A good example of this process can be shown using mirror neurons. It has been discovered that the same neurons that take part in planning a hand movement are also responsible for observing the hand movement of others. Lachmann and Mafessoni tried to figure out what would happen if the same process of understanding would be extended to any social interaction. After modeling outcomes rooted in the cognitive simulation, they discovered that actors responsible for as-actor simulation produce different systems typically explained in terms of kin-selection and cooperation. They also realized that an observer could once in a while coordinate with an actor even when the outcome is not beneficial. Their model is of the opinion that empathetic systems do not evolve only because animals or people simulate others to envision their actions.

According to Mafessoni, empathy must have originated from the need to understand others. For Lachmann, their discoveries have completely changed how people perceive and think about human beings and animals. Their model is based on a single cognitive mechanism that unites a wide set of phenomena under a single explanation. It consequently has theoretical import for a broad range of fields such as cognitive psychology, evolutionary biology, neuroscience, anthropology, and complex systems. Its power emanates from its theoretical interest and unifying clarity in the limits of cooperation.

Electromagnetic Fields

The subsequent finding depends on the way that both the mind and the heart produce electromagnetic fields. These fields transmit data about individuals' musings and feelings. Empaths might be especially delicate to this info and will, in general, become overpowered by it. Correspondingly, you frequently have more grounded physical and enthusiastic reactions to changes in the electromagnetic fields of the earth and sun.

Enthusiastic Contagion

The third discovering which upgrades everyone's comprehension of empaths is the wonders of the enthusiastic virus. Research has shown that numerous individuals get the feelings of people around them. For example, one crying newborn child will set off a flood of weeping in a medical clinic ward. Or then again, one individual noisily communicating nervousness in the work environment can spread it to different laborers. Individuals generally get other individuals' emotions in gatherings. Ongoing research expressed that this capacity to synchronize states of mind with others is vital for proper connections. What is an exercise for empaths? To pick constructive individuals in your lives, so you are not brought somewhere near pessimism. Or then again, if, state a companion is experiencing a hard time, play it safe to the ground, and focus yourself.

Expanded Dopamine Sensitivity

The fourth discovering includes dopamine, a synapse that expands the action of neurons and is related to the joy reaction. Research has demonstrated that contemplative empaths will, in general, have a higher affectability to dopamine than extraverts. Fundamentally, they need less dopamine to feel cheerful. That could clarify why they are increasingly content with alone time,

17

perusing, and reflection and need less outer incitement from gatherings and other enormous get-togethers. Conversely, extraverts long for the dopamine surge from happy occasions. Indeed, they cannot get enough of it.

Synesthesia

The fifth discovering, which is very convincing, is the original state called "reflect contact synesthesia." Synesthesia is a neurological condition wherein two unique faculties are combined in the cerebrum. For example, you see hues when you hear a bit of music, or you taste words. Be that as it may, with mirror-contact synesthesia, individuals can feel the feelings and impressions of others in their very own bodies as though these were their own.

This is an excellent neurological clarification of an empath's involvement. "Sympathy is the most valuable human quality." During these upsetting occasions, it is anything but difficult to get overpowered. All things being equal, compassion is the quality that will get you through. It will empower you to regard every other person, regardless of whether you oppose this idea. Sympathy does not make you a wistful softy without wisdom. It enables you to keep your heart open to encourage resistance and comprehension. It may not generally be successful in breaking through to individuals and making harmony but always believe that it is the most obvious opportunity you have.

Where Does Empathic Power Come From?

The question of where empathic powers come from, or how people come to possess them, is one that science still does not have a solid answer for. But there are a few theories. There is certainly plenty of evidence to suggest that a "normal" degree of empathy is accessible to most all of us in early development. Newborn infants in neonatal units display an inability to distinguish personal feelings from those around them. If one infant begins to cry, usually most others will follow suit very quickly as they are not yet aware that this pain or anxiety isn't theirs to own. Most infants who receive a healthy amount of care and attention will continue mimicry and emotional enmeshment throughout the first few years of life. This is how children are able to learn speech and movement. Some children, raised in especially tight-knit families or communities, may struggle at first to understand the function of pronouns that distinguish between the individual self and the group, posing questions like, "Mama, why are we sad today?" when they observe this emotion in another person.

Those who believe in the supernatural possibilities of empathic power also tend to believe that certain individuals are fated to receive these gifts and that empaths feel as they do in order to serve some greater purpose as determined by cosmic or holy design. This belief often coincides with the notion that empaths are born special and not shaped by their surroundings. While the level of power they possess or the manner in which they channel energy may fluctuate throughout their lives, their heightened sensitivity is considered an innate trait.

Conversely, there are those who believe empathic abilities come from the environment or circumstances in which a person is raised, as a function of nurture rather than nature. Many psychologists note that children raised in volatile, neglectful, or dangerous households learn early on to detect subtle changes in their parents' behaviors as a necessary coping skill and defense mechanism, allowing them to predict, avoid, or even prevent traumatic episodes.

Parents may not necessarily be nefarious or malicious in raising a child who develops extreme empathic sensitivity. Some theories posit that the only environmental factor needed to trigger such a development is an older authoritative figure in the child's life, who requires the child to empathize with them frequently. For example, a parent who is grieving the loss of a loved one might, without ever intending to, compel their child to empathize with a level of emotional pain, which they haven't yet been prepared for, and can hardly even comprehend at such a young age. A child who is put in this position frequently enough may never learn to distinguish their own emotions from those of others and might even struggle to feel that they are real, solid, or whole without the influence of another dominant personality. They become hyper-focused on caring for the parental figure in their life, and never learn how to receive care without guilt, shame, or anxiety, as most children do.

Once a child develops this ability, it is only natural for them to continue using it outside the home, amongst friends, colleagues, lovers, and even strangers. There are also those who note this same skill of hyper-sensitivity emerging for the first time in full-grown adults when they are romantically involved (or otherwise closely bonded) with an abusive personality type, like a narcissist.

It is worth noting that many empaths first become aware of their heightened sensitivity during relationships with those who are empathy deficient. Furthermore, whether they are aware of their abilities or not, empaths are so frequently involved with narcissists, sociopaths, and psychopaths. This makes many wonder if empathic power functions as a sort of invisible beacon to those who have these personality disorders. This theory—that empaths and empathy deficient types are drawn to each other like magnets—begs the question, which typically comes first? The empathic power, or the abusive environment in which it becomes a necessary skill for survival? While it makes sense that empathic abilities develop as a response to abuse and trauma, it is also certainly possible that abuse and trauma would always exist anyways, and empaths are simply drawn to these environments more than most people. An unfortunate reality of life for the empath who has not yet fully awakened to their power is that they will often feel compassion for those whom everyone else has abandoned, failing to see that these souls have been left alone for a good reason and are not worthy of the empath's care or attention. This could indicate that abusive circumstances and relationships are like traps which empaths are particularly vulnerable to falling into, rather than the cause or catalyst for heightened sensitivity.

Thus far, science has not been able to provide proof one way or the other, but some recent findings may allow for both possibilities to coexist. The study of epigenetics concerns the way in which our genetic material is impacted by our experiences and surroundings, meaning that we pass on more to our children through our DNA than simply a blueprint for the body. With the discovery of epigenetics, we are now able to theorize that trauma can have an intergenerational ripple effect, leaving a lasting mark on the descendants of victims, whether those descendants are fully aware of the trauma or not. This would allow a soul to be born with empathic abilities which are at once innate and a developed response to abuse.

There are many possible sources of empathic ability, and new information is constantly surfacing to expand our understanding of it. Likewise, the scientific field has yet to firmly define the source of empathy-deficient personality disorders, nor that of conditions like autism and Asperger's syndrome. Some believe these emotional states or conditions feed into one another, like two species sharing a symbiotic relationship, or an active embodiment of yin and yang energies. Others still believe there are purely biological explanations for conditions that fall on both ends of the empathy scale. Then, of course, there are those who see the empathy scale as a circle rather than a line, believing that a person with an overabundance of untrained empathic ability can evolve into a narcissist or vice versa.

Whatever you believe, one thing is clear: Empathic ability must be understood, trained, and balanced in order to be part of a healthy, happy lifestyle.

Chapter 2: Types of Empathy

Empathy is defined as the capacity to understand or feel the emotions of others. It can also be described as the ability to share the feelings of others. Empathy, for the most part, is a beautiful attribute. It's one of the finest qualities a human being can possess. It is associated with goodness, charity, compassion, care, and self-sacrifice. Empathy makes it easier to identify with those who are suffering, and consequently, take action to remedy the situation. The world can always do with a little more empathy.

Empathy is mostly classified into three groups:

Emotional Empathy

Here you experience the feelings of other people: sadness, anxiety, joy, pain, and so on. An emotionally empathic person catches the sensations of others, which strengthens relationships with those around her/him. Emotional empaths can do well in fields like medicine, nursing, and counseling since they deeply identify with the suffering of others and go out of their way to alleviate that.

The downside to emotional empathy is that your emotions fluctuate up and down, depending on the situation of those around you. That can be exhausting. In other instances, you feel the pain of others so deeply, yet there's nothing you can do to change their situation, and you're left suffering as well. In the following chapters, we will explore measures that empaths can take to protect themselves from such extremities.

Cognitive Empathy

This is the ability to know the thought process of other people, and in the process, understand their perspective. It mostly involves thoughts, intellect, and understanding. Cognitive empathy helps you appreciate different viewpoints. You're able to accommodate people who hold different opinions and beliefs from those of your own. This ability also comes in handy during discussions since you understand the thought process of others and engage them appropriately.

Compassionate Empathy

In this case, you do not only identify with the suffering of others, but you're also moved to take an extra step and lend your help. This is the ideal form of empathy, where you actually take action to make a difference.

However, precaution should be taken so that you do not run yourself dry, trying to donate to every cause. A donation here refers not only to finances but also time, expertise, skills, goodwill, and so on.

Empathy isn't just towards people. It applies to situations as well. An empath will be drawn towards the state of the environment, economy, politics, international relations, animal welfare, and such other matters that eventually affect the quality of human life. People without empathy find it easy to look away, especially when others are suffering.

First, all empaths are born with the ability to experience what other people are going through, either through emotions or even their feelings. Secondly, no empath is born already skilled. They all have to learn the skills, and if not, they are prone to suffer a lot. This should not get you worried if you have no skills yet, this book will help you learn some new skills that you need to know as an empath. To your surprise, you might even be more than one kind of an empath, so if you find yourself falling into various kinds of empaths, count yourself talented. These types are also referred to as the many gifts of empathy.

Physical Intuition

These are the kind of empaths who are able to know what exactly is happening in another person's body. For example, this type of an empath can easily tell when you have a stomachache or a headache. Being a skilled empath will make you able to help other people through this correct knowledge.

Physical Oneness

The way these empaths get information is always personal. These are empaths who can feel other people's physical way of being in their own body when around or with them. For instance, this kind of empath, when with Betty, they will always develop a stomachache, like this stomachache belongs to Betty. This is a confusing type of empath, but if you are a skilled one, you will be able to assist those around you with the messages you get into your body. You ought to be skilled to avoid confusion or any form of suffering.

Intellectual Empath Ability

These types of empaths are able to get into people's intellectual abilities. For example, they might find themselves using long words while speaking to Joy, but then later, they come to realize that Joy also likes using long words.

Emotional Intuition

These types of empaths are able to tell what is going on in someone's body, specifically their emotions, even when other people are trying to hide or fake their emotions. For instance, an empath will note that Betty is always cheerful, but she is hiding worries behind her smiles. Skilled empaths will know how to cut through the fake and real emotions since they all have the ability to differentiate what is real and what is fake. This helps you become a better friend since your friends get to realize you know them better.

Emotional Oneness

This is the type of empath where you get to learn the reality about what is cooking in other people's feelings. The difference of this kind of empath with the Emotional Intuition is that an empath in emotional oneness is able to feel what others are feeling. Your emotions and those of your friends will tend to merge. And as a skilled empath, you should not be carried away by the absorbed emotions since most of them are always negative. Instead, you should help your friends come out of this negative emotion or feeling, for instance, worries or anger. Being skilled means, you will have a stable emotional foundation to help out.

General Types of Empaths

Spiritual Intuition

This is a kind of empath where you get to experience how someone else connects to God or other spiritual beings. For instance, accompanying Betty to church and getting to hear what her pastor preaches about God, you get to feel the flavor that Betty gets from the teachings about God. This can happen in the case where you know nothing about your friend's religious views. Skilled empaths use this chance to know the many faces of God and even develop interests for religions and spiritual lives.

Spiritual Oneness

This kind of empath is different from that in Spiritual Intuition in that, in Spiritual Oneness, an empath will experience directly how their friends are connecting to their Supreme Being. This can be through the hymns that are being sung and relating the inspiration behind them. This helps skilled empath grow more spiritual in various ways.

Animal Empath

An animal empath will experience what it feels like to be a certain animal. A skilled animal empath is totally different from an animal lover in the sense that an animal empath is able to tell the difference between two animals that an animal lover thinks are identical. A skilled empath will help animals locate their groups or even help pet owners.

Environmental Empath

Environmental empaths are able to tell the difference between landscapes in certain environments. To them, each landscape is scenery. Skilled empaths enjoy walking through forests, and this can even make them emotional.

Plant Empath

Plant empaths get to feel what it is like being a certain tree, leave, or even flower. Skilled empaths use this gift in their agricultural farms or even in gardening.

Mechanical Empath

Mechanical empaths experience what it is to be a certain machine and their needs. This can even make them fix machines without the necessary qualifications due to the increased interest in machines. As a skilled empath, you are advantaged because you will not need a mechanic to identify what your machine needs, you will be able to tell it yourself. It may lead to more research into machines and technologies.

Medical Empath Talent

This gift helps identify any sickness or anything about your own or other people's health matters. Skilled medical empaths help give support, can even end up developing professional skills and become nurses, or even help in preventing any burnouts.

Empath Talent with Astral Beings

These empaths have direct experiences with astral beings such as angels and fairies. Skilled empaths will use the experience to grow themselves or enjoy more of these adventures.

Chapter 3: The Traits of an Empath

Most empaths have a hard time getting hold of their emotions. Can you imagine how much more challenging it is for a child? If you're an empath yourself, then you'll feel that your child is an empath. Most parents are not, so at first, they'll simply notice that their child is different. Here are some traits of child empaths:

- **They are Overwhelmed in Crowds**

While other children are happy to interact with others and jump around in crowds, empath kids will be fussy at best. Yet you can't blame them. All their senses are alert. They can hear every sound and smell every scent. Above all, they feel the emotions of those around them. They have a combination of feelings inside them: joy, sadness, anger, fear, and whatever else those around them are feeling. This is overwhelming for anyone, much less a child. The children will be uncomfortable and probably ask to leave. If you've not understood their personality, you'll be wondering why they can't enjoy the gathering like everybody else. If you cannot leave, then let them take breaks. You can have them sit in the car or in an isolated corner for some minutes. This helps relax their minds and emotions. With time, you should be able to identify the triggers and avoid or at least minimize them.

- **Cry when Others Are in Pain**

As soon as others are in distress, they will be in tears. This includes animals. They will offer to soothe those who are crying and end up crying as well. These kids can't stand to see others being bullied. They will cry along and try to beg the aggressors to stop. You know how it goes in these bullying cases. The kid supporting the one being bullied also ends up in the same boat. If your child comes home complaining about bullies, seek to find out the details. Perhaps your kid is being targeted for standing up for others. If you notice such a trend, chances are, you're raising an empath. Such kids should be encouraged. Those are the activists of the future. Assure them that they're brave to be standing up for others. They will only be picked on for some time, but once they prove their resilience, no one will dare bully others in their presence.

- **Excess Feelings**

Children have shallow feelings. If you upset them, they'll only be sad for a couple of minutes before something distracts their attention. That's why sometimes a child will get spanked then offered candy. The sadness evaporates in a minute. If your child seems to have intense feelings, especially the negative ones, you could be dealing with an empath. You may have spotted a video clip that was doing rounds online of parents pranking their kids. For most of them, they got upset for a moment when they realize they've been pranked. Then a moment later, they are giggling and promising to prank back. But there was this one kid that fell into a fit of rage. He shouted and cursed even as the dad explained that it was supposed to be a funny joke. That is definitely not normal for a child. A child will hardly ever be upset for hours. If you're dealing with such a case, chances are you're raising an empath. As a parent, help them acknowledge their feelings and walk through them.

- **Readers and Deep Thinkers**

Young empaths often have their faces buried in a book. They're seeking for information. They mostly read books that are beyond their age. They're interested in the real world, as opposed to fairly-tale stories. They think deeply about issues. They ask a lot of questions, the kind you would not expect a kid to ask. They question things that other people may not; like religion. *Who created the world? God. Who created God? He was always there. Everybody has to have come from something. And how could one person create so much?* The questions may irritate you, yet they will not relent. If you can't answer them, direct them to someone who can. If you always react with irritation, they will feel guilty and end up suppressing their curiosity. This curiosity ought to be fanned, not deflated. Such children could be grand researchers in the future, and who knows what they might come up with.

- **Sensitive to Media**

Empathic children get extremely upset at certain scenes in the animations or movies that they're watching. These are not a 2-minute frowning, but a complete change of mood that may even be accompanied by crying. They stay upset for a long time. The scene is likely to be one of a person or animal getting assaulted in a way. The kids feel deeply for the victim, never mind it could be a work of fiction. Since they cannot do anything to help, they release their emotions the best way they know how; by crying or sulking. Other kids might laugh at the empaths. To them, it's all fun and jokes, and they don't see why anyone should take it too seriously. If you notice that your child is highly sensitive to the media, monitor what they watch. Let them avoid content with intense scenes. Let them know that there's nothing wrong with what they feel, and their emotions are valid.

- **They Love the Outdoors**

This lot loves to get their hands dirty. They want to be out there exploring the outdoors. Since they feel with all their senses, they see so much where others don't. Your simple backyard feels like a nature trail to them. They will play 'fetch' with the dogs, build tree houses, dig around for worms, and plant a garden and pretty much anything else that crosses their mind. They will observe, feel, smell, touch, and basically have a blast out there. To you as a parent, you see them getting dirty. But they feel refreshed in those activities. The best you can do is let them explore safely. Buy books that teach them more about nature. Referring to the point about their sensitivity to the media, the outdoors becomes a great alternative.

- **Often Stay Alone**

Children normally reach out to others to play. Empathic children want to spend a lot of time alone. They will be in their room reading, exploring something, or just having a quiet time. If they have to share a room with a sibling, they will make an effort to carve out their own private space by forming an enclosure with a bed sheet or something similar. If you have playhouses, they will crawl in there and stay for hours. And no; they're not upset. In fact, they leave their little private spaces feeling better than before.

Do not force them out of their quiet sessions. Let them stay until they're ready to come out. Do not force them to play with the others either. If they seem reluctant, leave them alone. Given their deep thinking, child empaths often feel like they don't belong with their age mates. Their activities and conversation don't spark their interest. They may prefer to hang out with older kids or even adults.

- **Animal Lovers**

This trait begins very young. You will notice an intimate attachment even with stuffed/plastic animals. They will carry them everywhere, and even attempt to feed and bath them. Should they break or tear, they will be beside themselves with sadness. They will put a bandage on the wounds.

When they come of age, and you buy them a pet, the bond will be even deeper. They will spend the most time with the pet; showing reduced interest in people. Their caregiving properties will begin to manifest. They will attend to every need of the pet. Should the pet get sick or injured, get ready to drop everything and run to the vet? The child will be so affected to the extent of interfering with schoolwork.

As they grow older, child empaths show interest in animals on a larger scale. They could want to know what goes on in animal shelters. They could start talking about adopting an abandoned animal. They also gain interest in wildlife and love to watch National Geographic and other such programs. Buy them books that teach them more about animals. This interest can be nurtured into a career or into advocacy for animal rights.

- **Artistic**

They gravitate towards one form or another of art. It could be painting, drawing, playing an instrument, singing, and so on. They see things in multiple dimensions. When they look at a drawing, they see aspects that a normal child may not. As a parent, whether you share this ability or not, you should encourage it. Buy them materials to practice the craft that they're interested in. Once in a while, you can sit with them and have them explain the motions behind their pieces. You may not get it, but that's fine. You can also enroll them for classes to perfect their art.

Art offers a noble outlet for their emotions. When they're feeling overwhelmed, they can turn to art to express themselves. In their drawings and paintings and sculptures will be an outpouring of emotions, and that's what makes them so unique.

- **They Feel Your Energy**

This is probably the most unnerving bit of raising an empath. These children mirror your emotions. If you're sad, so are they. If you're going through a rough patch where you're experiencing mostly negative emotions, you can imagine the suffering the poor kids are going through. If there's strive in your family, such as a strained marriage, the children can feel it. You will try to act all fine in their presence, but they can feel every single emotion going through your body.

This makes them very sensitive. Children should be protected from adult challenges. If you're having a spat, you can send them to a relative for a few days. Do not let children suffer over an issue which they can do nothing about.

Their ability to feel also implies that you cannot lie to your children. In most cases, this happens the other way around. It is children who cannot lie to their parents, as they can see right through them. Here the roles are reversed. You cannot lie to your child that all is well between you and the other parent. They can feel the strain. You can't claim to be okay when you're sick; as parents often do to keep their children from worrying too much. They can feel your emotions, and in some cases, they can feel your symptoms in their own bodies.

The solution here is to tell them the truth. Tone it down to a language that they can understand. If you keep insisting on bending the truth yet their intuition is telling them otherwise, they will have a problem trusting you even in the future.

Raising an empath is no mean feat. It takes a while to understand what is happening to your child. You could even end up thinking that something is wrong with him/her, especially due to the time spent alone instead of playing with the others. The first step is to familiarize yourself with what being an empath is all about. Now that you're already reading this book, you're definitely on the right track on getting the relevant information.

That your child feels your energy means that you have to hold yourself to high standards. If you're plagued by sadness, anxiety, fear, and so on, your child will experience the same. These emotions are tough to handle even for an adult. Imagine how much more a child will struggle to try to manage them.

If you're going through a tough period in your life, for the sake of your empathic child, get help. Unfortunately, you do not have the privilege of handling your issues quietly. The moment you feel it; it's out there.

After working on yourself, concentrate on helping the child understand the unique personality. Many empaths will tell you how confusing it was as a child to be highly sensitive, yet not understand why they were feeling the way they were. Now that you're enlightened, your child should have better luck.

If children do not get this information in good time, they think that something is wrong with them. They suppress those emotions and numb their intuition in an effort to be normal. They suppress the urge to stand up for others, fearing they will be teased by their peers. With time, the gift goes to waste.

Let those around your child know that they're dealing with an empath. Start with the siblings. It can be challenging to have one child who is an empath and another who is not. They'll be wondering why they're so different and why they're not interested in the same things. Teach them about personalities as soon as they're in a position to understand.

Empaths are the minority in society, and if you have one in your hands, then you're one of the chosen few. Help that young empath to nurture that gift, accept it, and utilize it to the highest levels.

Chapter 4: Understand Your Empathic Nature

Empathy plays a key role in the functioning of society. It promotes our needs, sharing experiences, and desires between people. Our neural networks are set up to connect with the neural systems of others to both see and comprehend their feelings and to separate them from our own, which makes it feasible for people to live with each other without always battling.

Empathy is quite vital as it helps us be able to comprehend and understand the feelings other people are going through so that we can be able to respond appropriately to their situations at hand. To a greater extent, it has been associated with the social behaviors with research supporting it, arguing that the more empathy then, the more one tends to help. Notably, an empath can also be able to inhibit social actions or even go to the extent of having an amoral behavior. For example, someone who sees a car accident and is overwhelmed by emotions witnessing the victim in severe pain might be less likely to help that person.

Importantly, having strong empathy can also lead to negative causes. Such strong feelings towards our family members; social or racial groups can lead to hatred between one another brought about by insecurity. Also, people who are skilled in reading other people's feelings can start using this opportunity for their own gains by deceiving the victims. They include the manipulators, fortune tellers, and psychics.

Interestingly, people with higher psychopathic traits show more utilitarian responses in events where there are moral dilemmas, like, footbridge issues. In this experiment, people have to decide whether to push a person off a bridge to stop a train about to kill five others laying on the track.

Measuring Empathy

Quite often, a self-report questionnaire is used in measuring empathy. Such types of questionnaires include the Interpersonal Reactivity Index (IRI) or Questionnaire for Cognitive and Affective Empathy (QCAE). In the process of measuring empathy, the person is asked to indicate how much they accept the statements that are set to help measure the different types of empathy that one might be having.

One will find statements like, "It affects me very much when one of my friends is upset," which QCAE test uses to measure the effect of empathy. QCAE plays a key role in the identification of cognitive empathy by the use of statements such as "I try to look at everybody's side of a disagreement before I make a decision."

With the use of this method, it was discovered that people scoring higher on affective empathy have more grey matter. Grey matter is said to be a collection of nerve cells in the anterior insula, which is an area of the brain.

This zone is regularly associated with directing positive and negative feelings by coordinating ecological stimulants—for example, seeing an auto crash with instinctive and programmed in essence sensations. Likewise, individuals utilizing this strategy to gauge compassion found that high scorers of sympathy had a progressively dark region in the dorsomedial prefrontal cortex.

The activation of this particular area takes place when there are more cognitive processes, and this included the Theory of Mind. The theory is the ability of one to attribute the mental beliefs to oneself and another person. The theory also accepts the fact that one has to understand that the other person has desires, beliefs, intentions, and perspectives different from theirs.

Can Humans Lack Empathy?

Several cases have proven that not all humans have empathy. For instance, walking down Minnesota, you bump into a homeless person shivering in the cold. You will notice that few people will express sympathy, empathy, or compassion for the homeless person. Most of the time, we have seen people expressing outright hostility towards such people. So, what could be the cause of us expressing empathy selectively? Various elements assume the role. How we see the other individual, how we characterize their practices, what we fault for the other individual's difficulty, and our very own past encounters and desires all become an integral factor.

Further, I have come to find that there are two main things that contribute to human beings experiencing empathy— and these are socialization and genetics. Going back to age and time, we get to understand that our parents have the genes that highly contribute to personalities, and this includes our propensity towards matters, empathy, sympathy, and compassion. Notably, our parents spent enough time with us socializing, we chat with peers, the society, and the community at large and this is enough to affect us. The interactions have so much to do with how we treat others, our feelings, and beliefs as they are a reflection of our values and beliefs instilled in us while at the early stages of life.

A Few Reasons Why People Sometimes Lack Empathy:

    a. We fall victim to cognitive biases

Cognitive biases are said to play a key role in the way we perceive the world around us. For instance, attributing the failures of other people to internal characteristics and blaming our shortcomings on external things or factors. With this type of biases, then it might be difficult or rather challenging to be able to see all the factors that contribute to a certain situation, and that means we won't be able to see the situation from another person's perspective.

b. We dehumanize victims

Quite often, we are trapped in the thought that people who are different from us have different behaviors and feelings from us. This is evident when dealing with people who are different from us. A good example is a time when we watch conflicts, fights, disagreements, and calamities from a foreign land. Then, we end up having less or no empathy with the thought that those suffering are fundamentally different from us.

c. We blame victims

It happens that people start blaming a particular situation or suffering on the victim for his or her circumstance despite them undergoing a terrible experience. Many times, people ask what the crime the victim had committed to provoke an attack. This tendency stems from the belief that the world is a fair and just place.

We can't brush away the fact that empathy at times might fail, but people usually figure out how to identify with others in an assortment of circumstances. This capacity to see things from someone else's point of view and identify with another's feelings assumes a significant job in our public activities. Sympathy completely permits us to be able to take our time and understand others and compels others to go ahead and take an action that will help the person who is suffering. Empathy is all about minding about another person.

Can Empathy Be Selective?

Previous researchers have found that human beings tend to be more empathetic for members belonging to their group, like the ones from their ethnic groups. For instance, one researcher checked the cerebrums of Chinese and Caucasian members while they watched recordings of individuals from their ethnic gathering in agony. They likewise watched individuals from an alternate ethnic gathering in torment.

A study by other researchers has also found that brain areas involved in empathy are quite less active when we are watching people undergoing pain for acting unfairly. When a person is watching a rival sports team failing, we can be able to see activation in the brain areas which are involved in the subjective pleasure.

It is good to note that in such times, we never feel empathy for the people who are not of our group. When giving rewards to members who aren't in our group, the brain involved in such activity was very active when rewarding the same ethnic group, but when watching people of other groups being hurt, the mind activeness remains equal.

At times, it is advisable to be less empathetic to be successful. To put this into perspective, when in a war, a soldier should have less empathy, especially towards the enemy who might want to kill them. From the explanation, it emanates that humans tend to have an implicated brain when they are harming others and have a less active mind if the act is justified.

Assessing If You Are an Empath

Here is a simple test that can help you know whether you are an empath or not. Go through it, providing a simple yes or no answer to each question.

- Have I at any time been labeled as sensitive, introvert, or shy?
- Do I get anxious or overwhelmed frequently?
- Do fights, yelling, and arguments often make me ill?
- Do I often have the feeling that I don't fit in?
- Do I find myself being drained by the crowds, and by that then do I mostly need my time alone so to revive myself?
- Do odors, noise, or nonstop talkers get me overwhelmed?
- Do I have chemical sensitiveness or low tolerance for scratchy clothes?
- Do I prefer using my car when attending an event or going to a place so that I will be free to leave earlier?
- Do I use food as my source to escape from stress?

- Do I feel afraid of being suffocated by relationship intimacy?
- Do I easily startle?
- Do I have a strong reaction to medications or caffeine?
- Do I have a low threshold for pain?
- Do I tend to be socially isolated?
- Do I get to absorb the stress, symptoms, and emotions of the other people?
- Am I mostly overwhelmed by doing several things at a go, and do I always prefer handling one thing at a go?
- Do I replenish myself generally?
- Do I need a long time to recuperate after being with difficult people or energy vampires?
- Do I always feel being in a better place while in small cities than the big ones?
- Do I always prefer having one on one interaction and small groups and not the large gathering?

You can now try to know who you are by calculating your results.

- If you agreed to at least five of the questions, then you are partly an empath.
- If you agreed to at least ten questions, you are at a moderate level.
- If you agreed to eleven or fifteen questions, then you are a strong empath with strong tendencies.

- If you have agreed to more than fifteen questions, then it's without a doubt that you are a full-blown empath.

The determination of your degree of an empath is important as it will make it easy for you to clarify the types of needs and the type of strategy you will need to adapt in a bit to be able to meet them. With the determination, then you will be able to find a comfort zone in your life.

Chapter 5: Merits and Demerits of Empathy

Are you that person who gets bored easily, disliking commitments and routines? Do you tend to feel like the stability and repeating the same thing over and overweighing you down? How about having issues in respecting the people who try imposing their will on you? A person who does this quite often may be made to feel guilty by being given names like a selfish and troublesome person. Do you always have dreams of visiting new places and doing new things? This is thanks to your creativity and having high levels of energy generally.

A person who is not aware of their status could find a day to day interactions with others being a source of stress to them. Empaths, who are not aware of the abilities they possess, might be inclined to start using alcohol, food, and drugs to cure their emotional stresses.

Due to the positive impacts that the empaths bring, I tend to believe that they are the medicine that the world needs. They have a profound impact on humanity with the understanding and compassion they possess. In the process of learning and understanding your talents, you will realize that you may enrich not only yourself but also the people around you. You will need to understand that it is an important skill to fully understand how to be able to take charge of sensitivities and also get to understand the specific strategies that you need to use in a bid to prevent empathy overload.

Merits of Being an Empath

Being empathic has inconceivable advantages, for example, more prominent instinct, sympathy, innovativeness, and a more profound association with other individuals. In any case, living in this condition of high sensitivity likewise accompanies its difficulties, for example, ending up effectively overpowered, over-invigorated, depleted, or engrossing the pressure and pessimism of others.

I cherish being an empath so much. I thank God for the gift of sensitiveness bestowed on me. I have a strong liking on being intuitive, having a feeling of the flow of the world's energy, getting to read people, and also having an experience of the deep feeling the life offers.

I came to realize that God has given us so many marvelous traits that we ought to use on our day to day lives. You will need to understand that God gave us a huge heart and wonderful instincts that allow us to be able to help our society day in day out and those who are less fortunate. Empaths are said to both idealists and dreamers. Other character traits that define us include being creative, deep, passionate, compassionate, being in touch with our emotions, and can always see the bigger picture. Empaths can be friends with other people due to their ability to appreciate their feelings. They are quite spiritual intuitive and can always have a sense of energy. They highly have much appreciation for nature and feel it as their home. They highly resonate with nature, forests, plants, and gardens and have a deep love for the water.

Empaths get energized by the water, may it be warm or cold, taking a shower or even if they live by an ocean. They do feel a solid bond if they own animals, you can find them talking to the animal as they are just humans. With such a strong bond to animals, then such people might end up being involved with the rescue of animals or animal communication.

Being an empath is a blessing as they are natural healers with the ability to gift healing energy to their friends just via the hands, voice, or having to play a musical instrument.

Being an empath is an advantage given that these people only need their sense of smell for them to enjoy food, flowers, beverages, essential oils, etc. An empath who works harder and manages to increase his or her sensitivity can even smell death or disease from a person or an animal. With such ability, it means that many lives will be saved.

Empaths have an advantage of sensing danger before it hits; this is done using their sixth sense. Isn't that amazing? Notably, empaths enjoy feeling greater highs than the other people who don't have sensitivity. This is despite them being prone to feeling low due to the much energy they get from other people. Empaths have greater enthusiasm towards life; they do experience joy and life itself with greater intensity. They are advantaged as they are always kind, compassionate, caring, and understanding as compared to the other people who are not sensitive.

Even though the people who are not emphatic feel quite uncomfortable for not spending time with others, the case is quite different for the empaths as they do love being alone as this is the time they need to balance and de-stress. Empaths use this time to recuperate, and this makes them much aware due to the time they spent alone.

As discussed earlier, this kind of people do have high levels of creativity in their lives, and this is not only in the art field but also in situations, experiences, and possibilities. They can see things prior and hence being at a point of conceptualizing. Many people might label this creativity of thought and processing as wrong, but you won't need to worry about that, it's a capacity of yours.

Empaths enjoy the advantage of being able to read emotional cues, and this makes them be able to understand other people better since they can understand what that person is feeling and how it will affect the person if their needs aren't met.

Due to their sensitiveness, they are said to be very good at sensing all kinds of nonverbal communication and indicators of physical needs and emotions. With this ability then they can be said to be having a talent for intuiting the unconscious mind as well as for being able to sense the need the plants, animals, human body and those unable to speak.

Empaths have the advantage of being able to understand the thoughts of people, their feelings and emotions, and this ability enables them to sense a lie from someone. They can easily understand when something is a matter despite the person insisting that he or she is fine but hurting from inside. Because of our heightened awareness, we can see through the false facades people up.

Empaths have an advantage when it comes to loving as their degree of love is said to be on another level. It is believed that coming up with a mutual understanding in a relationship has proven itself to be a very hard thing. Empaths try as much to explain their feelings to the other person but unfortunately, they don't understand their feelings as the empaths do. It can take someone a lot of time for them to be able to place themselves in the shoes of the other person.

Through this, an empath can cultivate that high level of love and compassion difficult for the other people to accomplish despite the much time they might have at their disposal. With deeper levels of love, understanding and relating with people becomes quite easy, even those you are most likely to disagree with.

Empaths enjoy the advantage of being very creative. This is part and parcel of all empaths as through their emotions, and they can express their levels of creativity. Empathic can channel their feelings into a piece of art. If you are in the space, you need to be in, and then your creations will be touching other people around you.

Let's say, for instance, and you are an older adult who is unable to dance or paint; creativity will be able to teach you more about yourself. I came to realize that I am so much creative, and it is then when I started having an open book near me. This has assisted me in understanding so much about who I am, the meaning of life, and the patterns.

Empaths do receive insights naturally. Every creation allows an empath to be much happier, and further allow pure essence to explore itself fully. You can consider commencing with 20 minutes every week and believe you me that you will never want to stop.

Another benefit enjoyed by empaths is the ability to find and understand their true selves. This means that they are quite authentic and always speak their hearts and minds out. In my career, I came to notice that so many people face challenges when it comes to this. More so, in the current generation, many people see authenticity as a norm. Most of my clients have expressed themselves to me, saying that they would find it quite hard to be themselves. We do build a substantial prison around us as a society. You will need to make use of the facts that you quickly feel to your advantage. Empaths can connect to the deepest parts of themselves if they allow themselves to be very free. Some of the activities that you can engage in when alone include writing journals, having a new hobby, and dancing to be able to realize your true self. The main point behind this is to help you explore the depths within you. After feeling comfortable about it, you can then share with your friends by being authentic.

Therefore, when having a conversation with someone, you should always state yourself out comfortably, and don't shy from saying it if you feel the need. It is always advised to be polite to others and not attar statements that might leave them hurt. This becomes easier when you decide to share what in the heart freely. Understandably, it becomes quite caring and loving when people do speak their hearts out. And if the truth from our hearts becomes offensive to the other person, then it indicates that their ego has interpreted the message as an attack. However, you have the responsibility to say what matters to you and do it lovingly and openly.

Empaths are said to be peacemakers. This is because they have the ability the outside surroundings more than the inner surrounding. And it is due to this that leads them to be able to forego their needs and focus on the other person's needs. Generally, these people are said to be less violent, less aggressive, and they always tend to lean more toward being a peacemaker than a troublemaker. They are always filled by an uncomfortable feeling the moment they are in a surrounding filled with disharmony. If they find out that they in the middle of a confrontation, they will seek ways in which they can resolve the matter as within the shortest time possible or avoid it altogether. When harsh words are thrown to them in defense, they tend to resent their lack of self-control. They will always opt to handle the matter and resolve it promptly. Have you ever been in a similar situation?

Empaths sensitivity is a gift and not a curse. These people have the advantage of having creative thoughts, and through them, they can become something great. Therefore, before you start cursing your heightened awareness, you will need to remember that some of these advantages you possess, and you will need to uncover them. It is high time you start majoring on your benefits and advantages as an empath as this will enable you to create a life in which you will be able to benefit greatly from your gift and not drain you.

Demerits of Being an Empath

The most and common challenges I've known and seen with my patients and workshop participants include the following:

a) They struggle with anxiety and depression

Anxiety, depression, and doubt have been known to stumble the life of empaths. I am not surprised by this if I consider how they are embarrassed by our society, given all sorts of negative feedback. Besides, most of the empaths have been brought up in unstable homes, places where emotional welfare is raged daily. It is from this point that most empaths have resorted to addictions in a bid to be able to cope with the emotional overwhelm.

b) They attract narcissists and are energy vampires

We will agree that being an empath hurts because it does. These people do sense everything that every other person feels. They become greatly affected by other people's emotions. They can feel the loss and pain the other person is going through. They can feel their tears and the tone soul hence being quite hurt. But people won't understand them.

The empaths will act as an emotional sponge as they attract all manner of emotions when they are in the bank, grocery store, office, and from the surrounding people. They get to absorb the energy of the people who have the same energy signature.

Even though they are quite active in intuition, once in a while, we all get into the trap of the toxic people. This is the time when we give room to narcissists and other energy vampires to take advantage of your kind and compassionate nature. They find it hard to detach themselves from such relationships. They are highly disadvantaged because they never let many people in their lives, but when they do, they tend to give their all, of which the other person might take advantage of their character.

c) They feel too much but may not know why

With so many emotions and information hitting them from all corners, it is quite easy for them to be confused at the end. They may be unable to differentiate what issue belongs to them and what they collected along the way belonging to other people. They are also disadvantaged by the fact that their moods get tampered with by the physical environment. A very lovely-looking home might instead their levels of anxiety due to inexplicable reasons and factors. Because these people spend a lot of time going through subtleties around them, they end up spending a lot of time out than in their bodies. There is a dire need for an empath to take time to center and be fully in their bodies, and thoughts as this is quite important. By doing this, they will be able to establish boundaries in their life.

d) They have jellyfish boundaries and get stung

One of the main things that empaths hate is to disappoint others. This is brought about by the reason that they always feel the emotions in them and firmly, and it's the thought of hurting the other person is what makes their anxiety levels soar. They will feel quite guilty if they have to say no. It is for this reason that they might tend to have jellyfish boundaries something which might be taken for granted by other people, hence hurting the empath.

Also, if a person is seeking help from an empath, and the situation is quite dire, the helplessness behind the plea will highly affect the empath triggering them to accept the request even if it would mean personal misfortune to themselves. For an empath to stop being disadvantaged, then they will need to learn how to turn people away by saying no to requests that might cost them so much.

e) They face challenges when winding down

Empaths go through a hard time as they try to transition themselves from high stimulation to solitude. Brains never stop buzzing after a very involving and busy day at work. It is due to this that the empaths won't be able to focus easily. It is for this reason that we get a sad mood, or we feel a strange feeling after we get home from work, event, or a party despite it being filled with fun.

Have you been a victim of any of the above challenges? Then it is good to understand that nearly every empath has felt the same. There is no need to be ashamed of your sensitivity. Your empathy has much positive than detrimental to the world, and it brings to light more so when you get to learn the skills to learn and cope.

f) System Overload

Empaths are much wired to notice all the happening around them; hence, they experience a lot just before they get overwhelmed. Every empath should build up a tolerance because they relate quite differently, and this helps them be able to be quite aware when their sensory are being overloaded, and due to awareness, they can then have time to release and discharge.

Sometimes you can't tell if an emotion or sense of bodily discomfort is your own or someone else's. Taking on other people's energy can cause a variety of physical and emotional symptoms in you, from pain to anxiety

g) Sustaining Intimacy challenge

Empaths do face real challenges when in a relationship. Look at this scenario: an empath will have that time he or she will want to connect with their partners deeply, both body, mind, and spirit. Yet, still, there are times he or she will be feeling like blowing up yarning for time alone so to refresh and breathe. They are generally neutral at giving but what about receiving?

h) Becoming overstimulated

Empaths can quickly feel like they do possess a raw nerve something which can make them burn out quickly, and this is caused by the fact that they think not to be having the same defenses as the other people possess.

Failing to have enough time for oneself every day will lead to them to suffer from the toxic effects caused by being overstimulated and also sensory overload.

i) They Feel things intensely

Empaths have a challenge when it comes to anything seemingly brutal. They actually can't be comfortable when watching a violent or upsetting movie may it be about animals or humans because they will be badly hurt in the process. These people can even find themselves carrying the weight of the world on their shoulders as they can be suffering from the pain they took after watching the news or feeling the pain of a loved one.

j) They experience emotional and social hangovers

If you are associated with many people on a day to day activities, then you might be quite overloaded by the end of the day.

k) They have a feeling of being isolated and lonely

Because the world might appear to be quite overwhelming, you might find yourself keeping yourself a distant away from the rest. In the end, people may view you as standoffish. Like many empaths, you may be hyper-vigilant at scanning your environment to ensure its safety, which others can perceive as a signal to stay away. Some empaths prefer socializing online to keep others at a distance, so there's less of the tendency to absorb their discomfort and stress.

l) Experiencing emotional burnout

The fact that people will be flocking to you to share their disturbing stories will surely be emotionally distressing. I used to wear a sign written "I can help you" ever since I was a small child. And this clearly explains why empaths will have to set boundaries in their life if they want to stop being drained.

m) Coping with increased sensitivity to smell, light, smell, touch, sound, and temperature

Empaths find loud noises and bright lights being quite painful. They do react with our bodies, penetrate and shock us profoundly. All the time an ambulance passes-by, I have no option but to hold my ear. Could this be the same situation as you? What are your experiences when visiting your friend who has a home workshop and maybe with a loud machine? I have come to realize that I can't withstand the explosive blasts of the fireworks. They do startle me so much hence reacting similarly like a frightened dog.

Scientists have resulted that empaths have an enhanced startle response because they are super-responsive when it comes to intense sensory input. Empaths do feel queasy if they are exposed

66

to strong smells and chemicals, such as perfumes and exhausts. Could this be a similar experience to you? Empaths are also susceptible to temperatures extremes and even dislike air-conditioned places. Scientists have proven that our bodies as empaths can also be depleted or energized when in quite intense weather, the likes of gusty winds, thunderstorms or snowfall. Empaths get much energized by a bright full moon whereas, other empaths with feel agitated by the same.

Chapter 6: A Deep Dive into Empathic Listening

One of the most profound qualities of an empath is listening. What makes it so special; yet we all listen to people on a daily basis? How do they do it that the rest do not? Here's how to listen like an empath:

❖ **Attentive Listening**

Dedicate your full attention to listening, without doing anything else on the side. Stop scrolling on your phone or computer, typing, eating, or playing music in the background. Turn your body to face the speaker and maintain eye contact. Nod as necessary. Observe the facial expressions, gestures, and general body language.

It is not enough to listen; it is just as important to let the speaker know that you're listening. This assurance makes it easier to open up. Have you had one of those conversations where the listener turns attention to something else midway, such as replying to a message? You then pose to give him/her time to finish the task. But alas; they tell you to proceed. 'Go on. I'm still listening.' In most cases, this will be someone senior to you, so you will have no choice but to oblige. You attempt to carry on with the conversation, but you're deflated. You don't speak as well as before. It turns out the quality of listening affects the quality of speaking.

In this regard, attentive listening encourages the speaker to open up fully. This is what separates counselors from the rest of us. No wonder they manage to get people to open up on issues they've kept inside for years.

Attentive listening in the workplace encourages productive communication. Workers know that they can go to their bosses and express exactly how they feel. Customers can also give their honest feedback.

❖ **Non-judgmental Listening**

Following the point on attentive listening, try to listen without forming an opinion on what is being said. Listen to understand— not to answer. If you let your mind wander, you'll begin to critique what you're listening to mentally. This changes your perception and affects your listening.

It is natural to lean towards judgment. We often do it subconsciously. You have already set standards in your mind regarding how people should behave when faced with various situations. Everything is in black and white; right or wrong. While you're listening, you're also trying to classify the decisions and actions in the story as either right or wrong. How much can be achieved with such an attitude? Not much. You will even miss out on some bits of information as you're busy adjudicating.

Be cognizant of your thoughts, so you can catch them whenever they turn away from the conversation. Instead of labeling actions as right or wrong, seek to know the circumstances leading there. Ask follow-up questions. The answers will help you identify with the speaker and understand why they chose to act the way they did. While at it, don't interrupt. It can be hard to get back to a line of thought once interrupted.

❖ Rephrase

We often judge because we feel the need to say something in the conversation. We end up saying something like, 'how could you take him back after all he had done to you?' which is just plain judgmental. Instead, you can rephrase what has already been said. Repeat what you have understood from the conversation in different words. 'So, he convinced you that he had gone for counseling and was now a changed man?'

Rephrasing keeps your thoughts from straying. You remain attentive so that should you have to reword something, you'll have gotten it right. Restating assures the listener that you're attentive and encourages the conversation to keep going.

❖ Moments of Silence

Silence in a conversation does not have to be awkward. In empathic listening, moments of silence are not only allowed, but also encouraged. Opening up about sensitive matters takes a lot of energy. The speaker may have broken down and cried at some point. The listener also needs time to absorb what has been said. In moments of silence, both catch their breath.

Observe the speaker during the silence. If a hand of comfort is needed, you can offer a pat on the back or a rub on the back of the hand. Ask a follow-up question when ready to continue.

Silence does not make you a bad listener. Resist the temptation to barge into 'salvage' the moment. Silence is actually a healthy part of communication.

❖ See Things Their Way

Non-judgmental listening encourages empathy, where you put yourself in the shoes of the listener and feel the emotions. Picture listening to a 20-year-old who is pregnant and the boyfriend has left her. From your point of view, it is easy to wonder how she fell for such a common mistake. *What's wrong with these young girls? Couldn't she wait until she was married? Or at least use contraceptives?*

That's your narrative. But what's her story? That she met someone she truly loved. And he looked responsible enough to start a family. She was certain that they would eventually get married. She had always looked forward to being a mother, anyway. And she made her decision on the backdrop of these assumptions. As soon as you look at the situation from than angle, you can feel her pain of betrayal, and guide her appropriately.

If you allow yourself to trivialize their issues from your point of view, you'll be quick to assert how many others have gone through those situations before. Chances are they've already heard that before. And most importantly, it does not make their pain any less. Stepping into their shoes allows you to empathize with your situation, no matter how minor.

❖ End on a Positive Note

No matter how awkward the conversation was, it should end on a positive note. Find something good that can come out of the situation. If you're speaking to a lady who has just come of an abusive relationship like in the conversation above, point out something constructive about the episode. For instance, she can now tell the signs of an abusive partner from the onset. She can share such information with others to help them avoid such relationships. She can also help those in abusive relationships or those who have just quit. In short, the experience equips her with the knowledge that she can use to impact society.

❖ Follow-up

The conversation should not end when the two of you part ways. The talk should be the beginning. A problem indeed shared is a problem half-solved. What about the other half? It comes in what is done after the problem is shared. Here we're referring to a case of counseling where someone comes to you with a problem. You might have made some recommendations on how to move forward. Were they implemented? Was there any noticeable change? Does the burden feel any lighter? Monitor the situation so you can know how to proceed from there.

Merits of Empathic Listening

How do you feel when someone listens to you attentively, patiently, and without judgment? You feel valued and appreciated. In a world that is so quick to judge, knowing that you'll not be judged will encourage you to speak your mind and heart.

Listening in this way also strengthens relationships. True bonds are formed between people who can talk about anything. It is a lonely world. Even with hours spent on social media talking to friends and strangers, many people do not have someone whom they can open up to about the issues going on in their lives. Setting yourself apart as an empathic listener will draw people to you, and you'll be a treasure to those you interact with.

Finally, empathic listening ensures that communication actually takes place because someone is actually listening. Very often, we have someone who is talking, but the would-be listener is either distracted or disinterested. The communication chain is broken midway. Follow the tips above to become an empathic listener and watch the relationships with people around you shift for the better.

When You Don't Know What to Say

After listening, you feel compelled to say something. Often, you don't know what to say. You may result in these cliché statements:

- God will see you through
- He/she is in a better place
- This too shall pass
- I know how you feel
- Don't worry; things will be fine

These statements are said in good faith, but they rarely help. Essentially what these responses are saying is 'things are not that bad.' They're belittling the person's predicament. In any case, he/she has already heard these statements before.

Remember, empathy is all about connecting with the other person's pain and emotions. You cannot show empathy by downplaying the situation.

Start by acknowledging their pain or struggle. This shows that you understand what they're going through; or at least that you're trying to. You can say something like 'I see how difficult that is' or 'that must be really challenging.'

Then, appreciate their step of courage in opening up. It takes a lot of guts to do so, especially if they've tried to open up before and received a negative response. Talking to you means that they trust you, and it pays to acknowledge that faith in you. 'Thank you for choosing to share this with me' would suffice.

Ask questions to prompt further information. People often begin to open up then stall midway, either due to emotions or just afraid that they've already revealed too much. Assist them to go on talking. 'How did that make you feel?' 'How have you tried to cope?' 'Anything else that you can mention on this issue?'

Finally, show support. You can't fix everything, but you can be there. Offer to listen whenever the need arises. Reinstate your love and care. Affirm them by reminding them that they're brave and strong enough to go through the situation. Such an empathic response will leave those who have the privilege to speak to you feeling better and boost their ability to deal with their situation amicably.There is no blueprint for empathy. You just have to follow your intuition, which is something that you're good at as an empath. Deal with each case as your inner voice leads. You will leave people feeling better, and you'll gain fulfillment from utilizing your gift of empathic listening.

Chapter 7: Protecting Yourself through Energy Healing

The way to self-care is to rapidly perceive the primary indications of encountering tactile over-burden or when you begin engrossing pessimism or worry from others. The sooner you can act to lessen incitement and focus yourself, the more adjusted and ensured you will be. At whatever point you begin to feel depleted or overpowered practice the accompanying five security tips.

❖ **Shielding Visualization**

Protecting is a snappy method to secure yourself. Many empaths and touchy individuals depend on it to shut out lethal vitality while permitting the free progression of inspiration. Approach it consistently. The moment you are awkward with an individual, spot, or circumstance, set up your shield. Use it in a train station, at a gathering on the off chance that you are conversing with a vitality vampire, or in a pressed specialist's lounge area. Start by taking a couple of, deep, long breaths. At that point, imagine an excellent shield of white or pink light encompassing your body and expanding a couple of crawls past it. This shield shields you from anything negative, distressing, harmful, or nosy. Inside the security of this shield, feel focused, glad, and invigorated. This shield squares out cynicism, and yet, you can, in any case, feel what is absolute and cherishing.

❖ Define and Express Your Relationship Needs

Knowing your needs and having the option to affirm them is a reliable type of self-security for empaths. At that point, you can be in your full power in a relationship. If something does not feel right, raise the issue with your accomplice instead of enduring quietly. Discovering your voice is proportional to creating your capacity; otherwise, you may end up depleted, restless, or feel like a doormat seeing someone where all your fundamental needs are neglected. Your accomplice is not a mind peruse. Talk up to shield your prosperity.

Ask yourself, "What do I need in a relationship that I have been hesitant to request? Okay, incline toward all the more alone or calm time? Okay, prefer to rest without anyone else's input at times? Would you like to play more or talk more or engage in sexual relations more? Or on the other hand, might you want to move under the full moon together? Give your instinct a chance to stream without judgment. Reveal your actual emotions-no motivation to be embarrassed or to keep down.

❖ Set Energetic Boundaries at Work and Home

Empaths frequently endure in their condition when they ingest the worry in their environment. The work environment mainly can be loud and over-invigorating. To ensure your vitality level in a sincerely requesting or swarmed condition, encompass the external edge of your space with plants or family or pet photographs to make a little mental obstruction. Sacrosanct articles, for example, a statue of Quan Yin (the goddess of empathy), the Buddha, hallowed dabs, precious stones, or defensive stones can define an enthusiastic limit. Clamor dropping earbuds or earphones are likewise helpful to mute discussions and sound.

❖ Prevent Empathy Overload

When you are retaining the pressure or side effects of others, and you have to discharge the negative vitality, breathe in lavender essential oil or put a couple of drops halfway between your eyebrows (on your third eye) to quiet yourself. When you are capable, invest energy in nature. Offset your alone time with individuals time. For you, time the executives are vital to your mental stability. You should make an effort not to plan patients consecutively.

In your own life, you do not design such a large number of things in a single day. You ought to have likewise figured out how to drop plans when you get over-burden. This is expertise. All empaths must adapt, so you do not feel obliged to go out if you are worn out and need rest. Set clear cutoff points with vitality vampires and dangerous individuals. Keep in mind, "No" is a complete sentence.

You do not need to continue accounting for yourself. You are brave about abstaining from depleting individuals, especially when you are over-burden at long last practice self-empathy. Be sweet to yourself at whatever point conceivable refrain from pummeling yourself. In the wake of a monotonous day, let yourself know, "I did as well as could be expected. It is alright nectar."

Activities That Can Help You Thrive as an Empath

❖ Express Your Thoughts and Feelings

Get into the habit of consciously expressing yourself when you feel something. It gives you the power to handle your emotions more effectively. This does not mean throwing a fit of rage or yelling at people or crying all the time. However, when you feel something, open up at least with people whom you can trust.

Do not get aggressive or act increasingly submissive. Gently stand up for your feelings without resorting to belittling or pulling down others. Assertiveness is taking charge of the situation and your emotions in a more constructive and calm manner, without doing things that will further damage the situation.

If you want to become more emotionally intelligent, start getting into the habit of taking control of the situation in a balanced and assertive manner without resorting to aggression or passivity.

Present your stand in a clear, non-offensive, and sure manner. You will eventually start becoming more confident, develop better negotiation/problem-solving skills, and manage anxiety efficiently.

❖ Identify Feelings without Judging Them

Tune into your deepest feelings and emotions without being judgmental about it. For instance, when you identify that you are experiencing pangs of jealousy towards another person, do not automatically term yourself or your feelings as bad or wrong. Simply acknowledge that there is a feeling of jealousy and try to tackle it more positively.

❖ Take Responsibility for Your Actions

Accepting complete responsibility for your actions is one of the first steps towards developing a higher emotional quotient. Emotionally intelligent people do not feel the need to shift responsibility on someone else, justify their wrongdoings, or defend themselves aggressively. They shy away from putting the blame elsewhere and completely own up to the mistake.

You acquire the ability to control your emotions, manage negative feelings, develop more fruitful interpersonal relationships, wield better decisions, and influencer your actions more positively. You are not relying on others or external circumstances for determining your emotions but taking charge of how you feel.

❖ Use Generous Doses of Humor

That thing about do not take life too seriously, no one gets out alive anyway is true to an extent, isn't it? We increase our stress levels by viewing every situation with seriousness and conflict.

Get away from that mindset consciously and start seeing things with a more light-hearted and humorous perspective. View the positive or optimistic side of every situation to keep the atmosphere more upbeat. Spread joy and happiness wherever you go. If the situation seems slightly tense, try to crack a joke to lighten the mood a bit.

❖ Master Empathizing with People

Emotionally intelligent people are adept in the art of feeling other people's feelings. They place themselves in other people's shoes to understand the other person's perspective. When you develop empathy, you learn to consider every situation from other people's point of view, too, before coming to a decision that benefits everyone. This understanding paves the way for less conflict and greater stability in relationships. Connecting with others becomes effective and more fruitful when you learn to acknowledge the feelings of others.

The next time you find yourself getting angry with someone, stop in your tracks, and try to understand why they may be compelled to behave the way they do. Is it related to their childhood experiences? Is it related to issues related to low self-confidence or self-esteem? Has an incident deeply impacted them? Try and pin down their behavior to underlying factors to gain a more holistic overview of the situation. This will help you handle the situation more intelligently rather than succumbing to impulses or thoughtless actions.

Chapter 8: Empaths, Insomnia, Exhaustion, and Adrenal Fatigue

As an empath, one should remember that his/her presence is a blessing; the sweetness and tender application of the gift of empathy on people make all the difference in the world. The special intuition and refined sensitivity are a healing platform for self and others. Empathy comes with loving, kindness, and compassion.

However, as seen in previous topics, empathy has a list of challenges. These challenges include; absorbing the negativity and stress of others, Becoming overstimulated, experiencing social and emotional hangovers, emotional burnouts, feeling things intensely, feeling lonely and isolated, the need for space even when in a relationship, and dealing with heightened sensitivity to light, taste, smell, temperature, touch and sound.

These challenges can hinder the performance of an empath, both physically and emotionally. The spiritual gift of empathy tends to become a challenge once a person forgets or fails to understand that the true purpose of this ability is to heal. Empaths might find themselves absorbing all the energy instead of using it to understand the situation without hoarding it. Consequently, the empath becomes overwhelmed by the emotions and in worse cases; he/she becomes physically and mentally ill. Uncontrolled empathy has been linked to conditions such as body aches, difficulties thinking clearly, adrenaline fatigue, insomnia, and exhaustion. It is important for an empath to remember that his/her energy source is not without a limit. Energy is finite; therefore, if an empath keeps giving without taking care of oneself, he/she will eventually run out of energy.

Empaths are like sponges that absorb the emotions, feelings, and conditions of those around them and as such, they can absorb an array of health problems, including physical conditions. This sharing of emotions leaves the empath very tired such that they need a lot of sleep/ rest in order to repair what has been affected. Unfortunately, many of the empaths find it hard to sleep and toss in bed all night. Consequently, these empaths do not get healed completely, and instead, they become broken down and depleted.

Researchers say that many of the empaths are misdiagnosed when they seek medical attention because there is little understanding of the empathy phenomenon in the medical field. People often say that if the world had fewer guns and more hugs, we would be living in a better place.

The society has been made better by empathy and empathetic people. As seen in previous chapters, empathy is one of the main keys to survival for both humans and most animals. We have lived through the centuries witnessing the kind acts of people such as Mother Teresa and Mahatma Gandhi. These people are considered empaths because they have gone beyond and over what other people can do for the world. We can say that without these people, the world could not be as bright as it is today. However, the energy it takes for one to give their heart, soul, and strength to another comes with a high price, and as such, most of the empaths find themselves dealing with burnouts and adrenalin fatigue.

Empaths can experience an unexpected onset of chronic fatigue because of the significant crash of different energy levels.

Mostly, this crash is a result of having an array of emotional responsibilities. Empaths leak their energy so furiously that it is almost impossible to remain grounded, consciously aware, and balanced. These people will mostly feel drained when they have spent too much time in the presence of others. Interactions with people can lead to emotional exhaustion for the empath. As such, the people with the gift of empathy need a whole deal of alone time to recharge their energy levels.

The thoughts, feelings, and emotions of empaths can play havoc on the internal systems, thereby causing devastating consequences that debilitate the people involved. IF THE empaths have regular moments of solitude within the day, then they get the time to process emotions and feelings, avoiding exhaustion. Taking some alone time facilitates better emotional, physical, and mental conditions because the empath is able to let go of the bad energy that might play on the mind and weigh him/her down.

If the empath does not get enough time to retreat and reenergize, if he/she lacks space during the day, then the mind will react at night. One might wonder why the mind chooses to overreact at night; it is because the night is still and quiet, meaning that there are no distractions from external stimuli. Consequently, these reactions make the empath unable to relax and allow sleep to take over.

In other cases, the empath may be able to sleep but will keep waking up throughout the night. The interrupted sleep sessions are as a result of the mind trying to process the information it over absorbed during the day. As the empath attempts to make sense of the occurrences that took place during the day, insomnia crops up. The consequences of insomnia include daytime sleepiness, irritability, low energy, and depressed moods.

The hyperactive mind brings about fatigue on the individual by continuously hurling an overwhelming amount of stimuli at the empath, not allowing him/her the chance to replenish rest, and recharge. Consequently, the empath will have erratic sleep patterns whereby some days he/she will need only two or three hours of rest while other days require ten or more hours of rest, depending on the amount of energy that is attached to the energy field and is pulling the person down.

If one does not find time during the day to figure out the internal thoughts, emotions feelings and commotion taking place within the mind, it is essential that he/she engages in meditation before sleeping in order to clear the mind enough to rest. Allowing thoughts to come and go lightly without paying too much attention to them allows one to get some closure without igniting a psychological response that is hormone-induced.

Our experiences and memories are linked to emotionally charged feelings that tend to provide emotions such as resentments, fear, anxiety, paranoia, and panic. Consequently, the human mind is convinced that the owner is under some form of genuine threat. This belief makes the brain to send signals to the adrenal glands to release hormones that facilitate a surge of energy.

When someone experiences prolonged or intense stress or anxiety, the lifestyle becomes very unhealthy. For instance, one might get into substance abuse, too much/ inadequate sleep, poor diet, overworking, stressful relationships, family challenges and general life crises-consequently, the individual places excessive continuous demands on the adrenal glands.

What are adrenal glands? They are small endocrine glands shaped like kidneys, approximately the size of walnuts that are placed in the area just above the kidneys in the lower back. These glands are essential and beneficial when one is under stress because they release hormones that keep the individual focused, alert, and creates increased stamina to facilitate better handling of stress.

However, when the adrenal glands are overstimulated, they keep producing energy which results in conflict, especially when we try to sleep or get some rest. Consistent overstimulation of the adrenal glands makes one feel like they are permanently wired on high alert. If a solution is not found in time, the adrenal glands experience excessive stress, and they might eventually malfunction and burn out.

As the energy levels get drained quickly, empaths are tempted to top it up with instant solutions; therefore, they will settle for quick fixes such as highly refined foods with high levels of sugars and salts. These foods burn energy very fast, giving an instant boost of energy. However, this move initiates a vicious cycle whereby the refined food burns energy very fast, leaving the person in need of more junk to fuel the body. When people feed the body with the refined products found in most quick fixes, the body only craves more sugar and salt because it thought it what it needs to keep it going. People should be having unrefined salts and sugars because these have high nutrition value, and when consumed in healthy doses, it can replenish and nourish the adrenal glands.

People might again try to raise energy levels by taking products that are high in caffeine, for instance, coffee and energy drinks. What they fail to understand is that caffeine just irritates the glands further. As a result, the consumer will experience regular lows and highs as the energy levels drop and hike throughout the day. When the adrenal glands are not working as they should, the affected person will feel constantly fatigued, anxious, irritable, overwhelmed, dizzy, and run down. Again, one might experience sugar and salt cravings, heart palpitations, low blood pressure, high blood pressure, and a harder time when dealing with stressful situations.

If one is well balanced, he/she thinks positively, eats well, sleeps and gets enough rest and as such, the adrenal glands are not easily overwhelmed. During sleep, the levels of cortisol in the body rise naturally and peak just a few hours before we wake up. This increase happens so that a person can have a good start once he/she wakes up. It is also referred to as circadian rhythm, and it elevates and reduces energies accordingly so that the body can function effectively by staying awake when it is daytime and sleeping when it is dark.

When the adrenal glands are exhausted, an empath and any other person for that matter wake up feeling tired and disturbed even if he/she has had a long and otherwise restful sleep. This person will feel drowsy for the better part of the day, and then the cortisol levels will rise in the evening. The late peak will result in a lack of sleep or difficulty resting at night. It is very hard for anyone who has overrun the adrenal glands to get them back to a normal state. It can take a lot of time, but there are some changes that one can make and have an immediate positive effect on the glands.

For an empath, the most critical initial thing to do is to listen attentively to the body and take note of how it feels. If one pays attention to the feelings of the body, then he/she will stay aware of how the energy levels within are rising and falling throughout the day. This will help in noting the hours during the day, which one feels exhausted than others; therefore, make the right moves to alter the patterns.

It is important that an empath understands why he/she is placing too much energy pressure on the glands. Once he/she identifies the root cause of the stress, emotions, and feelings, it will be easier to ensure that a heightened state of alert is brought down, therefore removing the pressure from the adrenal glands.

In some cases, the empath may have to use medication to help focus on the body in order to identify any sensation that is taking place. Medication can also help one to soothe the mind and become calm so that he/she does not keep repeating the negative thoughts that will trigger adverse chemical reactions.

Another method that can help one to regulate the level of cortisol is spending time with friends, family, and outside, doing social activities. Scientists have found that cortisol levels increase if one spends too much time alone. Loneliness, separation, and isolation trigger feelings that we associate with negative experiences; therefore, empaths should learn how to balance alone time with social time. Consequently, cortisol will not be such an issue.

Other factors that affect the cortisol levels include diet and exercise. The regime that one uses for exercise and feeding determines the amount of stress placed on the adrenal glands. If one pushes the body too much, then he/she places too much demand on the adrenal glands, which then results in an overproduction of stress-related hormones. Bad practices such as skipping meals, intense workouts, and eating junk foods force the glands to overwork. In the event that the person has food allergies, then the glands get additionally stressed. As such, it is vital to be attentive to the food that one tolerates.

An empath can keep the adrenal glands nourished and balanced by sticking to a healthy diet and getting enough exercise. An organic, nutritious, and well-balanced diet with healthy levels of proteins, and vitamins A, B, and C can go a long way in ensuring that the glands are functioning properly. It is also important to allow time for the body to absorb the nutrients before a person can engage in any physical activity. The empaths can also avoid large consumptions of alcohol and eliminate the intake of refined products and caffeinated foods.

If the unrest and sleeplessness occur due to disturbances in the mind at night, then we can create an environment that helps rebalance the glands. For instance, one can create stability, security, inner peace, joy, and optimism just before going to bed. The aim is to get a restful night's sleep, and sometimes we can be startled by the thought of going to bed and failing to drift off as expected. Anxiety develops just before getting to bed when one realizes that he/she is going to stay awake for hours without getting to the highly desired delta state. The anxiety only makes matters worse.

When the adrenals are exhausted, empaths tend to wake during the night on high alert and to make matters worse, high stimuli dreams can add to the overanxious state of mind. Sleepless nights are particularly common for the empaths after they have endured an anxious and stressful period. When they enter sleep, they can keep waking up at intervals during the night because of the hormones circulating through the body even when they cannot understand the cause.

Disturbances in sleep are in most cases linked to biochemical reactions resulting from the flashes of high levels of stress hormones occurring throughout the body system between 2:00 AM and 4:00 AM. The high spike of these hormones affects the body so dramatically that it becomes impossible to remain calm; thus, the ability to stay asleep is interrupted. These disturbed sleep challenges can be rectified by making a therapeutic potion that consists of unrefined salts and organic honey. Mix one teaspoon of unrefined salt, for example, the pink Himalayan salt with five teaspoons of raw organic honey. The salt has healing properties, while the honey supplies the body cells with energy. One can take a teaspoon of the mixture about 20 minutes before sleeping; it will help to relax the mind and naturally regulate hormones. Consequently, one will be ready to drift into a restful place of rest.

Summary of Techniques to Deal with Adrenal Fatigue, Insomnia, and Exhaustion

It is easy to understand how being empathetic can lead to constant exhaustion, insomnia, and adrenal fatigue, especially if the person is frequently around a big crowd. After empathizing, socializing, and taking in all the emotions and feelings in situations such as this, most empaths need time to recuperate and recharge their energies. They will require a quiet environment to heal.

If the person cannot identify a time during the day to sort out the thoughts and feelings, he/she will be forced to deal with the issues at night while trying to sleep. The quietness and calmness of the night make it easy for the mind to keep analyzing things it took in during the day.

Consequently, the empath will wake up unrested and fatigued; therefore spend the day worn out. This will definitely become a vicious cycle because in the evening again, the mind will start to drift. The adrenal glands will be producing hormones when they are not needed and failing to reach the expectations when needed. The crash of energies makes the empath more confused, tired, stressed, fatigued et cetera.

However, the empaths can help their bodies to get the rest they need by taking a few positive steps. For instance, they could use more natural sources of salt and sugar which will supply the body with long term energy, therefore, breaking the cycle of the need for instant energy from refined products. Again, becoming more active helps one to replenish the adrenal glands. If possible, one should gain and maintain a positive attitude towards life; the benefits will increase mentally, physically, and emotionally. With these simple practices, an empath and any other person should start to notice an increased amount of sleep and proper rest, revived levels of energy, and overall happiness in life.

Balance the time spent alone with the time spent with family and friends. It is very beneficial to balance socialization. Get into activities that make you happier; for instance, ride a bike, nature is good. Watch an inspirational movie. There is always something to learn. Follow a nature trail. Fresh air helps to open up, unwind, and get clear thoughts. Boundaries are also very essential for dealing with fatigue and exhaustion. One of the main challenges of empaths is that they will always want to help; thus, they forget that their energy has limits. Boundaries will help one to avoid the manipulation of energy vampires. It is okay to say no and also to rest.

Meditation has also been noted as one of the techniques that makes life easier for the empaths. Meditation makes one check into their bodies and minds and heals the things that are broken. For empaths, meditation also helps to identify and eliminate the emotions absorbed from others. One can meditate for about ten minutes in the evening to release the stress collected during the day, therefore creating room for sufficient sleep and rest.

Exhaustion, insomnia, and adrenal fatigue are bad for the health of any person, regardless of whether they are empaths or not. Good adrenal health is essential for everyone; therefore; we should share the information about the glands with everyone. Wearing out the adrenal glands leads to a lot of health issues. Although empathy is a gift that should be shared as much as possible, one should find time to take care of him/herself. And to keep going, it's important to pick the habit of practicing a positive mentality. This means patting oneself on the back for achievements and not beating oneself up with negative thoughts.

Chapter 9: Enjoy your empathy

Regardless of our empathic abilities or lack thereof, we all aim to fill our lives with as much joy as possible. Using the tools and strategies outlined in previous pages, the empath should find that their overall level of happiness generally increases. As it becomes easier to recognize and manage the different types of energies that surround them, it will also become easier to be selective and make consistently positive choices.

Still, even for those who have mastered these skills and choose to focus all of their energy on positivity, constant and everlasting joy is an unrealistic goal to strive for. We all have our blind spots, vulnerabilities, and weaknesses. Sooner or later, the empowered empath will encounter a source of negativity that they cannot (or simply do not wish to) ignore, compartmentalize, or remedy.

It is in those moments, where joy is not accessible, that the empath must learn to find a way to inner peace instead. Imagine, for example, that someone you love and deeply respect has passed away. It would be ludicrous for anyone, even an empowered empath, to expect to find their way to true joy during the funerary services, or at any point within the mourning period. Whatever your views on death and the possibility of an afterlife may be, a loss of this magnitude is always painful. If the empath wishes to attend a wake or funeral, they'll certainly need to prepare themselves for the experience. They have to utilize whatever strategies they need to avoid taking on the pain of other mourners in the room. However, the empath who is focused exclusively on seeking joy may run the risk of ignoring their own genuine feelings of pain, thereby distancing the self from emotions and feelings that belong to no one else. This is a dangerous practice for any empath to grow accustomed to, as it can be seductively pleasant at first. But much like the alcoholic who avoids the pain of a hangover by consistently consuming the hair of the dog that bit them, the empath will find that they can never outrun their own emotions. Even if they aim to shut them out the same way that they shut out the feelings of negative people, the emotions almost always find their way back to the empaths.

Balance, ultimately, is a superior goal. An empath with a strong sense of inner balance can attend a funeral, commiserate with others, and honor their own sadness and process feelings of grief without being consumed by them. Their balance allows them to recognize that sadness is not an opposing force to happiness, but rather that it is a functional part of joy; that without misery, we would never feel bliss or perhaps anything at all.

Over time, the empath will learn that this state of equilibrium is indeed their most heightened state of being and the place where they will find their truest self.

Learn how to deal with discomfort

Here's a revolutionary idea that can take your yoga, tai chi, or mindfulness practice to the next level: discomfort is just an emotion. It isn't real. It isn't a threat, but it is a motivator.

Embracing discomfort isn't the same as numbing yourself to it. When you accept cognitive dissonance or moral injustices, you numb yourself to discomfort, embracing apathy, and encouraging the distortion of the truth. When you allow yourself to experience discomfort without immediately reacting, however, you can learn to make empowered choices, overcome fears and anxieties, and reach towards emotional growth. For empaths, discomfort is often a sensation of uncertainty or anticipation of conflict. If you can learn to recognize the feeling without letting it trigger your fight or flight response, you can instead focus on taking productive action, making yourself the true master of your own universe.

This is an enlightened position that very few humans take. If you can start to use your discomfort as a tool, rather than avoiding it at all costs, you may find yourself able to overcome challenges that leave others destroyed. Once you've mastered this technique, do your best to pay it forward to another empath.

Live a comfortable life

One thing that can throw any empath off balance and block the pathway to inner peace is a lack of authenticity in your lifestyle. Empaths often carry lies or dishonesty inside for long periods of time, haunted by them, even allowing the memory of them to block their throat, heart, and solar plexus chakras. This being the case, it's best for empaths to avoid lying whenever possible--even white lies can cause disruptions in your energy field.

You can work towards this goal through both addition and elimination. In addition, make a point to invite positive energy flow into your life by aligning your career, personal relationships, eating habits, and hobbies with your value system. For example, if you have come to realize that environmentalism is deeply important to you, then pursuing work in green planning would be a fantastic first step. You could also reach out to foster new friendships with people who are passionate about the same causes. You might alter your diet to favor organic, locally sourced produce, and make a heightened effort to buy from environmentally conscious companies.

For elimination, you'll want to start purging anything from your life that puts you in a position of moral conflict. If your job or social circle is not environmentally conscious, you'll be under constant pressure to swallow your truth and project dishonesty, which will ultimately leave you feeling dissatisfied and ungrounded. Any relationship wherein you feel the need to lie to keep everyone happy is a bad relationship for you, and you should feel free to let go of it.

You'll also want to stop using your money to support brands whose values contradict your own, and give up any habits that have a negative impact on the things that matter most to you—for instance, if you love poetry, song, and other forms of vocal expression, it's may be time to quit smoking cigarettes once and for all. You might be pleasantly surprised to notice your physical body and metaphysical energy shift in a tangible way once you release the cognitive dissonance you once held inside yourself. You'll feel lighter, taller, more dynamic, and more capable.

I'll include another reminder here to be careful with social media use. Sometimes, these applications can do a lot of good to bring people together and inject dynamic momentum into progressive movements—but most often, they are cesspools of inauthentic energy. Aim to use these platforms sparingly, if at all, and to post honestly and responsibly.

Choosing Humility and Respecting the Unknown

No matter how empowered one may become, and regardless of how well one has honed their empathic power, it is important to embrace humility and keep the mind open for unexpected possibilities. The self-righteous empath who develops a hermetic view of the world, unwilling to entertain ideas that do not strongly resonate with their interior knowledge, is likely to be deeply discontented or anxious, and struggle with communication and loving relationships, as others will perceive them to be arrogant and standoffish.

This type of attitude is also likely to weaken your empathic powers. Truth is multifaceted and always changing. In order to grasp even a sliver of it, the empath must maintain a balanced connection between their interior and exterior worlds. Shutting either out, or favoring one over the other, will eventually lead the empath to receive misleading messages, or lead them to misinterpret messages that would otherwise be clear and easy to decipher. Empaths are privy to knowledge that often goes unseen, unheard, unacknowledged, but from time to time, they can be flat out wrong, especially if the information they're receiving from the exterior world is limited, it can be skewed to support an incomplete hypothesis.

There is an ancient Indian parable, of possible Buddhist origin, that has become popular in discussions of philosophy and religion, spreading to cultures throughout the world and retold in several different versions, about a group of blind men who encounter an elephant in the jungle. (Perhaps this parable is due for a modern update to include an equal number of blind women. Please bear in mind, men are not the only gender susceptible to the pitfalls this proverb warns us against.) In this story, each of the blind men must use only their hands to try and comprehend the elephant's size, shape, and overall nature; however, one man's hands find only the elephant's tusks, while another finds only the rough skin of a hind leg, and another still can only feel the animal's wide, thin ears. When they compare their experiences, they are each convinced that the others are wrong or insane; in some versions of the story, this inability to agree on their sensory perceptions leads the men to resort to violence. Ultimately, the point of the story, which only the audience can see, is that each of the blind men is right, describing his experience accurately and honestly; the only problem is that they fail to acknowledge the perspectives of others as equally valid.

This is human nature, though the parable aims to inspire us to evolve past it. The truth can never be fully comprehended from one fixed vantage point. It is far too vast for any single person to hold alone. Still, the enlightened empath will be more successful than most at gathering contrasting perspectives and finding a way to incorporate them all into a single philosophy or belief, untangling knots of cognitive dissonance and drawing connections between seemingly disparate concepts. If, and only if, they are willing to stay humble and open to uncomfortable experiences, that is. This pursuit should be handled with care—again, there is a difference between mild discomfort and decisively negative energy. And it's important for the empath to stay guarded against the latter. Don't force yourself to endure an experience that is depleting rather than charging you, but don't let yourself fall into the habit of avoiding the challenging and unpredictable opportunities life offers you, either. As an example, many empaths learn early in their journey to self-empowerment that large crowds can quickly cloud or drain their energy fields. They may have had one particularly difficult or painful experience at a party, concert, funeral, wedding, or rally, and quickly decide that it would be best to avoid large gatherings from that point on. This might be a mistake, though, as joining large groups that are unified in honest intention (a faith-based service, or performance that is effective at steering the emotional path of every audience member, for example) can be one of the most positive and energizing experiences available to the empath.

Though it may be tempting to stay cocooned in whatever emotional spaces feel safest, the empath must make a point of continuously expanding their perspective by trying new things, meeting new people, and seeking out challenges for the sake of growth. The most important thing for any empath to know is just how much the universe has yet to teach them.

Chapter 10: How to Protect Yourself from Energy Vampires

An energy vampire is quite a harsh phrase here. It is used to refer to people who always want things their way while disregarding everybody else's feelings. These are toxic people who do not care about the emotions of others, provided their interests get served. Energy vampires are bad for everyone, but particularly for empaths.

Empaths are ready givers, while the energy vampires are ruthless takers. If you're not careful, they'll drain you dry, and you'll have no energy left to take care of anyone else, including yourself. Common symptoms of energy vampires include:

- Insecurity makes them feel disadvantaged. They complain all the time, outlining their perceived challenges in great detail. You're forced to walk on eggshells around them, to avoid making their situation any worse. Having such a person around you is like having a fussy baby, just without the sweet face.

- They demand attention by claiming always to have a crisis. Even when good things are happening, they find a way to turn the situation around and see a problem there. And you don't dare claim to be having a problem as well. Yours will be promptly be declared trivial. Theirs is always the most serious issue in the room. They thrive in the 'poor you' attention every single day, whether the problem is real or imaginary. Playing victim demands that other people lift them with their energy, which can be tiring.

- They never take the blame for anything that happens to them. It's always other people's fault. If they're flagged for non-performance at work, it's not anything that they did wrong. It's their coworkers who don't like them. Or the boss that is picking on them. If their relationship goes wrong, they won't point out what they could have done better. It's always the other person. Or other people who are jealous of the relationship. If there's no one to blame, even the good old universe is not safe. 'No one likes me.' 'Nothing good ever happens to me.' Here they're trying to say that the universe has conspired against them. How convenient?

- The spotlight always belongs to them. Should anyone else try to occupy it, especially with a happy story, it is instantly grabbed back. They will pour cold water on your happy news. You could have just gotten engaged, but instead of celebrating with you, they will talk about divorce statistics. They will remind you that 60% of all marriages end up in divorce. They will tell you of their peers who got engaged in glamorous weddings and didn't even last long enough to celebrate their first anniversary. These statistics may not even be true. They're simply intended to bring you down. Alternatively, they'll turn the story around to be about them; how they were once engaged, but so-and-so left them heartbroken. Now the attention turns to the sorry story. They never embrace joy and thrive in deflating the joy of others.

- They guilt-trip you into doing what they want. They will make you feel like it's your fault that they're miserable. They will say things like 'it seems I'll just have to go through this on my own. Everyone treats me like crap. You don't have to invite me. Nobody invites me anyway.' You will feel sorry for them, which is exactly what they want. You will then go out of your way to accommodate them, even when that means jeopardizing your own welfare.

- Their opinions are made to sound like facts, and in their usual character, it will be negative. They will say something mean about your hair or clothes, with zero regard to how it makes you feel. 'You're going out wearing that?' The question will be asked in a sneer. You will be left feeling judged, mocked, and ridiculed. They will expect you to go right back and change; that's how highly they think of their opinion. Be ready for the second round of scrutiny even when you change, the alternative might not be good enough either for their taste. Or something will be wrong with your shoes this time. They also criticize things that you cannot change—your height, the shape of your nose, or your personality. They leave you feeling miserable and are too self-absorbed to care.

- They speak of worst-case scenarios to spread fear. They can't stand positivity, so they'll always bring up those things that make people anxious. *What if we lose our jobs? What if the economy crashes? Do you know how much toxins are in these packaged foods? Have you checked the statistics on cancer cases?* If there is nothing bad happening, they will bring up that possibility. And that sight of your frightened faces will further cater to their twisted egos.

Dealing with Energy Vampires

Energy vampires are well amongst us—friends, family, colleagues, and peers. You can't avoid them completely. Your paths will cross at one point or the other. As an empath, keen to share goodness with all and sundry, you may be tempted to play the bigger person. You may even look for a way to help them change their ways. But remember that these people are thieves of energy, and of joy. They will leave you so deflated that you'll not have the strength to serve others, much less yourself. They will waste your gift. You have to engage them with caution.

Are energy vampires intentional, or do they do so by chance? There are those whose character is flawed by experiences. They grew up among energy vampires. They don't know how to be happy. They're accustomed to misery. They simply treat people how they were treated. This lot has a chance of changing if somebody points out the negative effects of this habit on others.

Then there are those who are vampires by choice. Life has dealt them a few rough cards. They're not happy, and they don't want to see anyone else happy. Instead of focusing on working through their situation, they choose to make others miserable so they can ride in the same boat. They know what they're doing, and they know they're hurting others. But they don't care.

Here's how to deal with energy vampires:

➢ **Set Time Limit**

If you're obligated to deal with them, set time limits. These are people who can engage you for hours if you let them. And the conversation will be dominated by their sorry stories the entire time. It's normal for people to have challenges, but you can't have this one individual claiming to be in crisis all the time. Set a time limit and let them know. For instance, you can say that you only have one hour to listen, after which you'll have to attend to something else. Be firm with your time limit; they will try to manipulate that too.

➢ **Avoid Arguing**

Contradicting an energy vampire yields nothing. They will come to you whining about a failed relationship claiming always to be innocent. You will try to make them see the part they played in the failed relationship. As usual, they will not accept any responsibility. They will only insist that they're innocent. Don't argue; otherwise, the conversation will carry on till kingdom come. Just listen to what they have to say. They're happy just to have your attention anyway.

➤ Be Brief

If you have to speak, stick to brief questions. Why? How? When? Such monosyllable questions will suffice. Here, keep your opinions to yourself. Voicing your ideas just keeps them going on and on, so they can discredit them and have theirs emerge as superior.

➤ Minimal Reaction

An energy vampire seeks to evoke an emotional reaction from you. They tell you their sorry stories, and they expect you to be sad for them. When they say degrading things, they want to see you angry and in despair. Do not give them these reactions that they're looking for. Remain passive. Listen with a straight face. Let them know that you're not moved by every whim. If your emotions fluctuate up and down as they engage you; they win. Don't let them 'win' at your expense. Nobody deserves that.

➤ Avoid Eye Contact

Empaths are good listeners and love to listen with all their senses. We have explained in a different chapter how empathic listening includes eye contact. If you're dealing with an energy vampire, however, this rule does not apply. Eye contact makes you more vulnerable to what is being said; just what we're avoiding here. Keep the eye contact to a minimum. Avoid sitting facing the speaker. Just glance at him or her occasionally. This does not sound very considerate but remember, you're dealing with a peculiar character here who is up to no good, and you have to protect yourself.

➢ Stick to Light Topics

We stated earlier that empaths thrive in deep conversations. Again, we have to make an exception here. You do not want to start speaking about the meaning of life with an energy vampire. They will do what they do best; water down your opinions, bring out their sad stories and create worst-case scenarios for everything. Make the conversation as light as possible. When they bring up issues of their own, just glaze them on the surface without going deeper. These are people intent on dragging you through the mud, and the closer you are to the surface, the better.

➢ Reduce Contact

Reduce the instances where you have to encounter such people. If they make a habit of popping into your home or office, let them know that they can only come with prior notice. What if they actually belong to your house or office? They could be your family members or workmates, you know. A bit tricky here; right? You still need to reduce contact. The last thing you need is an energy vampire siphoning your energy in the place where you spend your most time. If you have such a workmate, you're not obliged to hand out with them. If you go for lunch as a group, you can choose a different café, or carry a packed lunch. Do not entertain idle talk at your desk. If you have such a person at home, spend more time in your room. Distancing yourself from energy vampires is not selfish; it is a matter of self-preservation.

➤ Be in a Group

An energy vampire inflicts maximum damage when you're alone. Invite others into the conversation. If you have a workmate who singles you out to listen to sorry stories, you can request to involve the others, so they can also give their input on the issue. If they hover around your desk in the office, request them to bring up the conversation during lunch. You know the rest will be present, and you'll not have to suffer as much. In addition, someone in the group could have the courage to stand up to the energy vampire and call him/her out. Expect an argument, but the toxic character might just think about it afterward and makes some changes.

➤ Disengage Completely

Empath as you are; you can only take so much venom. Some energy vampires will be relentless, never stopping for a minute to think of the consequences of their actions. You will try to make them see some sense, but they'll be too self-centered to listen. You have a rare gift, which should be influencing as many as possible. You cannot afford to entertain people who will deflate you and makes it nearly impossible to serve. Feel free to cut off links. The world out there will teach them better.

Energy vampires deplete you physically and emotionally. You can actually feel changes in your body for every minute that you listen to them. You may feel sweaty, breath shallowly, have a faster heartbeat, and even experience a headache. Emotionally you feel anxiety, despair, and panic and even lose focus. You have that gut feeling that warns you that you're spinning out of control.

These effects could continue even after the toxic person has left. You keep replaying their words in your mind, and you feel drained all over again. It takes a while to detox from that feeling. Now imagine if you encounter several of these characters. You'll be so drained, with no energy left to attend to anyone.

You cannot afford to entertain this lot. What's worse; you won't even help them. Remember their goal was not to solve anything; it was to get attention. Their thirst for attention is like a bottomless pit. It's never enough. You do not have to suffer as a result. Remember, you cannot help everyone. The best you can do is hope that they decide to change, for their own good. Use these tips to tame them so you can go ahead and be of service to many others.

Chapter 11: How to Control Your Emotions with Meditation and Grounding

❖ **Returning to Earth**

As an empath, you have consistently been to some degree 'ethereal' in nature. Being ethereal can feel rather happy, far-reaching, and free – an invited alleviation from the power of being an empath. The ether is the space where unadulterated vitality thrives. It is the place life-power, chi, nourishment, widespread life vitality streams. Since empaths are about energy – feeling, detecting, transmuting and vibrating vivacious frequencies – the ether is somewhat an asylum for delicate creatures. It tends to resemble washing in an ocean of light. It is serene, quiet, and unlimited. Etheric vitality is a language that empaths get it. It just bodes well. It feels like home. For you, being ethereal ought to consistently be the simple part. Being encapsulated and grounded as a person, in any case, while feeling and detecting the majority of the energies around you is all that you need!

❖ Gliding Around and Crash Landing

Try not to be accustomed to being grounded by any means, frequently feeling floaty without a stay. You can be imbued with a mind-blowing feeling of softness, yet you could thump somebody over with a plume. This is the place the issue may begin from. It can bring about ceaseless 'crash arrivals' – back to earth! These unexpected, brutal shocks can even send you in turn. You may feel overpowered and thoroughly washed through with disorderly energies, an inclination that is so natural for empaths. Without being grounded, it tends to be hard to release the strengths that you had accepted. Without a firm ground to remain on, you cannot understand that feeling of steady quiet that usually happens when anybody is earthed.

There may be a moment that it occurs to you that without imbuing your experience of being an empath with an Earth association, you could be merely drifting around like a tumbleweed in the breeze; which is all great. However, it cannot generally fill a need. Your otherworldly encounters can be astonishing, with the most dominant of acknowledging; yet you could be floating. You may understand that your endeavors to acquire the heavenly and genuinely fill your need can be pointless except if you give it a firm ground to arrive upon. In this way, you ought to before long become familiar with the imperative significance of being grounded.

Why Is Establishing So Significant for Empaths?

One of the issues that empaths and exceptionally sensitive people face is feeling exhausted and fatigued because we take on an excessive amount of vitality from outside of ourselves. Here is the reason establishing is significant.

- Grounding offers a moment approach to release undesirable energies
- Grounding bolsters you enthusiastically
- Grounding reestablishes and revives your vitality field
- Grounding advances a moment feeling of quiet
- Grounding improves mental, passionate and empathic clearness
- Grounding gives your life's motivation someplace to arrive

❖ **The Mother Earth Association**

Even though you may feel the profundities of empathy for Mother Earth, being grounded does not work out efficiently for some Empaths. It is typically a procedure that must be educated. The brilliant incongruity for you could be, that regardless of your tendency towards the etheric domains, Mother Earth can be probably the best motivation. With the unlimited love of a genuine Mother, she can continually be close by, controlling you through this manifestation. You could not need to request a superior instructor. She addresses each individual, managing individuals with her antiquated shrewdness – all you have to do, is tune in.

Physical bodies are made of similar stuff that Mother Earth is. In this sense, individuals are all likewise offspring of the Earth (regardless of were known to humanity individuals feel they may have recently originated from). When you go out into nature, your vivacious recurrence starts to sway a similar recurrence as the Earth. This breathes life into you. It inhales everybody. It reestablishes and revives your vitality field. The reappearance of Mother Earth is amazingly mending. It is superbly designed for an ideal person.

❖ Getting to be Earthed

Studies have since found numerous methods for establishing. The best is regularly the most basic. Strolling in nature is fantastic, just as anything that encourages you to feel your bodies (that is, moving, development). You may find that being shoeless and touching the ground underneath your feet, in a split second revives your proclivity with the Earth. You may love to invest energy interfacing with anything familiar; communing with the trees; venerating untamed life; feeling the loftiness of the moving slopes and mountains.

Basic Hints for Establishing

- Acknowledge the significance of creating for yourself
- Commit to intentionally interfacing with nature at whatever point conceivable
- Use a reflection to enable you to ground and interface with Mother Earth

An Establishing Reflection

(While regarding your etheric nature)

Here is a straightforward technique for establishing any place you are – regardless of whether you are not out in nature. In this reflection, individuals additionally respect your unique ethereal quality as well. Preferably, locate a particular spot, associated with the Earth, in any case, if you cannot do that where you are at the time, envision your association with the ground.

Close your eyes and carry your attention to your association with Mother Earth.

Feel your vivacious 'roots' sink into the Earth, through your feet (if standing) or base chakra (whenever situated).

When you feel associated, get a feeling of Mother Earth unadulterated vitality ascending through you. Enable her spirit to stream up through your base, permitting the implantation of Earthly energies all through your body.

Feel the completion of your body as you feel grounded and associated with Mother Earth.

Allow your ethereal self to imbue into your body while keeping up your feeling of 'groundedness.'

Your ethereal and natural energies will start to move together and inject.
Carry on with your day feeling the completion of your groundedness. Feeling alert, associated, present, and mindful.

As an empath, this will keep up a feeling of yourself, without getting excessively lost in other individuals' energies.

Grounding Methods to Help You Center Yourself

These days, with the consistent assault of negative energies, it is a test for the Empath to remain grounded. Notwithstanding when staying at home, inside their asylums, their empathic radio wires are continually exchanged on, getting passionate vitality from the outside world. Along these lines, they effectively become depleted, overwhelmed by disregard, and diverted from their actual Empath jobs. To battle the consistent overpower, the cutting edge world engravings on an Empath, they have to secure themselves and work to remain grounded. Everybody is extraordinary, and what works for one Empath won't generally work for another. Be that as it may, it must be stated, the best type of assurance and approach to remain grounded for any Empath is to make a flexible, solid body, calm personality and solid vitality field. The following are probably the ideal approaches to accomplish this:

❖ Water

The body is comprised of seventy-five percent of water (somebody tissues have ninety-five percent), so it should not shock anyone this is far up there on oneself mending scale. Numerous individuals are unconscious of exactly how got dried out they are. Lacking supply of water makes issues with the working of the enthusiastic and physical bodies, influences general prosperity and quickens the maturing procedure. Water is a fantastic defender for the Empath, and they need loads of it, both inside and outside of their bodies. Most ought to drink in any event eight glasses of unadulterated water multi-day to recharge what the body usually loses through perspiring or pee. The heavier you are, the more water you need. There is an old religious saying that: 'Neatness is an underdog to righteousness.' Water washes something other than earth away; it can rinse the animated body and evident cynicism. If you are doubtful, when you get back home from a hard day at work attempt this: rather than going after the wine, bounce straight in the shower and see what an elevating and clearing impact it has. Or on the other hand when feeling genuinely fatigued beverage a half quart of lukewarm crisp water and perceive how it weakens the effect.

❖ **Diet**

Perhaps the best thing an empath can do, for establishing as well as for all-round equalization, is to incorporate all the more establishing, nutritious sustenance to their eating routine and evacuate any medication like nourishments. Wheat is one of the most exceedingly awful guilty parties. Stopping a long story: grain acts as a medication in the body. Empaths respond more to medicate like nourishments than those not of a delicate sort since they are profoundly receptive. High reactive are sensitive to various vibrations of vitality. Everything is vitality vibrating at multiple frequencies, and that incorporates sustenance, medications or liquor: the quicker the wave, the higher the recurrence. Empaths are contrarily influenced by anything of a low vibration. Most drugs and alcohol have low vibrational vitality and cut the Empath down quick. Wheat is not classed as a medication, even though it demonstrations like one, and in this manner conveys a similar mark. You may not eat bread but rather still devour loads of grain. It is covered up wherever for a reason it keeps everybody swallowing a more significant amount of it.

❖ Sea Salt

It is said that the 'father of drug,' Hippocrates, was among the first to find the, practically otherworldly, mending capacity of ocean salt, after seeing how rapidly seawater would recuperate injured anglers' hands. In addition to the fact that sea is salt an incredible restorative healer, it is additionally profoundly decontaminating. It can draw out and break up negative energies from the passionate and physical body. This is particularly useful if your day includes interfacing with others, where over and over again, you wind up picking their pushed or on edge vitality. Salt is not establishing, for the Empath, yet an immensely valuable vitality clearing apparatus.

How to Balance Your Energy

By adjusting your manly and female vitality, it works exceedingly well to help keep you grounded and enthusiastically steady.

❖ Smudge

Smearing helps clear your Empath vitality field of undesirable vitality and furthermore offers extraordinary insurance.

❖ Exercise

In the Western world, many go to practice for the advantages of weight reduction and a conditioned body. Be that as it may, the practice offers quite a lot more, particularly for the Empath. It discharges repressed feelings, evacuates debasements through perspiration, improves and elevates states of mind, stimulates, expands joy, assembles a ground-breaking vitality field, and is likewise establishing. With regards to exercise, do what you adore. If you do not care for guidelines, schedules, or set occasions at that point, go free-form. Make the principles yourself. Get the music turned up and move like no one is watching (which it is most likely best if nobody is while tossing shapes out). Move, stretch, and bounce your considerations away and get a sweat on.

❖ Meditation

This is an absolute necessity on the off chance that you have a bustling head with interminable personality gab and dreadful musings, as most Empaths do. A bustling disordered personality is un-establishing. Reflection encourages you to manage distressing circumstances and gives you a more precise understanding. There are numerous types of contemplation. It is only an instance of finding what suits you.

Example: The Jaguar Protection Meditation

126

When you need additional security studies to prescribe this reflection to approach the intensity of the puma to ensure you, you should utilize it when there is an excessive amount of antagonism coming at you excessively quick. The panther is a savage and patient gatekeeper who can ward off dangerous vitality and individuals. In a quiet, thoughtful state, from your most profound heart, approach the soul of the puma to secure you.

Feel her essence enter. At that point, envision this flawless, incredible animal watching your vitality field, encompassing it, ensuring you, keeping out interlopers or any negative powers that need to get past. Picture what the puma resembles: his or her lovely, wild, adoring eyes; smooth body; the agile, intentional way the panther moves. Have a sense of safety in the hover of this present puma's security. Give inward gratitude to the panther.

Realize that you can approach her at whatever point there is a need. Feel the intensity of that. As a touchy people, you should learn the way to manage tangible over-burden when an excess of is coming at you too rapidly. This can leave you depleted, on edge, discouraged, or debilitated. In the same way as other of us, you may feel there is no on or off switch for your compassion. This is not valid. When you think ensured and safe, you can assume responsibility for your sensitivities as opposed to feeling defrauded by them. To pick up a feeling of security, perceive some regular factors that add to sympathy over-burden. Start to recognize your triggers. At that point, you can rapidly act to cure a circumstance.

❖ Creativity

In a universe of standards and schedule, individuals only here and there persuade time to be imaginative; however, this is perhaps the most straightforward approaches to delight in the high vibe factor. When you feel great, you likewise feel grounded. When you make from your interests or interests, it has an inspiring impact on your mind, and when participating in something you adore, it wards off the brain from dull contemplations and sentiments which is an unquestionable requirement for all Empaths.

❖ Chakra Balancing

You have seven primary chakras which are a piece of your enthusiastic body. They are your focuses of otherworldly power that run the length of our organization, from the lower middle to the crown of the head. The chakras are spinning vortices of vitality lined up with the endocrine framework (organs which emit hormones, for example, adrenalin, cortisone and thyroxine into the body). At the point when any chakra is out of equalization, it can make infection (dis-ease) inside the body. Discovering approaches to adjust the chakras assists in being establishing just as being extraordinarily advantageous to the strength of the body and psyche.

❖ Yoga

Numerous individuals claim that yoga is not for them, yet it is the very individuals who get some distance from yoga who are the ones that need it most. Yoga is fantastically establishing. It takes a shot at the physical and lively bodies and serves everybody, regardless of what age or capacity. Yoga ought to be a staple in each individual's life. There is a yogic saying that: 'We are just as youthful as the spine is adaptable.' Because yoga attempts to make a supple spine, it could be classed as a mixture of youth. The very center of yoga is based on the breath. By taking all through stances, it stills and quiets the psyche, and makes a solid, supple body. Yoga is likewise classed as a moving reflection.

❖ Nature

Being outside in life has a recuperating and establishing impact on each Empath. As an Empath, on the off chance that you invest little energy in kind, you will battle to remain grounded or discover balance. If you work in a city, with no entrance to parkland, ensure you get out at ends of the week from autos and air contamination.

❖ Laughter

As adults' individuals invest a lot of energy being grave and genuine, and too brief period having a ton of fun (particularly in the present occasions). Do you recollect the last time you had an appropriate paunch snicker? Imprint this, 'You do not quit playing since you develop old; you develop old since you quit playing!' You hear youngsters snicker always. They do not have a clue how to pay attention to life; it is about play and fun, which helps keep them grounded. Everybody ought to endeavor to remain untainted. To see the world in surprise or more all have a ton of fun and chuckle. Anything that makes you giggle will make your spirits take off. It truly is a treatment.

❖ Crystals

The mending intensity of precious stones has for some time been known in various societies, from Atlantis to old Egypt. It is accepted that the people of yore had costly stone chambers they used to mend physical, profound or lively infirmities. Precious stones can be utilized related to the chakras to help balance them and expel blockages. Detecting their normal mending vibration, many Empaths are instinctually attracted to precious gems for their establishment and defensive capacities.

* **Essential Oils**

As with gems, the mending intensity of first fuels has been known through the ages. It is through the olfactory faculties that a large number of the advantages of essential oils are gotten. There is an organic oil to suit each Empath for either: assurance, establishing, re-adjusting, unwinding, and that's only the tip of the iceberg.

* **Earthing**

Even though this is a late expansion to the rundown, it is one of the most useful with regards to Empath establishing. Earthing includes setting exposed feet on characteristic earth or strolling shoeless! You may frequently underestimate the remarkable recuperating intensity of Mother Earth yet associating with her is perhaps the simplest ways for the Empath to discover balance. Blocking out the unwanted emotions of others

So how would you quit engrossing other individuals' vitality? How might you disperse negative life?

* **Discover Your Unresolved Issues**

You do not need to concentrate on what other individuals are doing. You need to focus on things that you need to fix inside yourself that other individuals feature in specific circumstances and conditions you face throughout everyday life. What happens when you get into a discussion with somebody, and you feel annoyed? They have hit a nerve which makes you need to lash out at them.

What have they done? They have gone about as an impetus to stir the dormant beast. It could have been some other individual in some other area. Indeed, you find that it is not so much the other individual as it is your uncertain issues. What is going to enable you to quit retaining other individuals' vitality, is to begin investigating those issues. Many individuals live from the outside in, so other individuals become their issues. In any case, when you start to live from the back to front, that is the point at which you begin increasing more exceptional lucidity. For some individuals, it is challenging to discuss uncertain issues since they would prefer not to assume liability. Everyone will be your concern until you begin investigating yourself and begin fixing your unpredictable problems, and start recuperating wounds to end up the total, and start reintegrating the divided pieces of yourself to turn into your most prominent adaptation.

❖ Express Yourself 100%

Convey what needs be without blame. What happens when somebody converses with you for quite a long time, and you need to state something; however, you would prefer not to be discourteous? You remain quiet. You become a wipe. You are presently retaining the majority of their vitality. By acting like this, you disregard your actual validness, and you quit liking yourself. In any case, when you can genuinely express 100% and expel blame from the condition, you build up a more noteworthy straightforwardness which will enable you to turn into your most remarkable form. Commonly the motivation behind why such a large number of individuals do not express how they truly feel is because they have been informed that their actual emotions do not make a difference. Growing up, individuals chipped away at the reward and discipline standards. On the off chance that you did things right, or regardless of whether you did what your folks needed, you would be compensated irrespective of whether you did not generally feel where it counts this is the thing that you needed to do. Everybody has a ton of quelled feelings. Concealment is wretchedness, and once you can communicate 100%, you begin to decrease tension.

❖ You Are Not Responsible for Others

You have no power over how other individuals react to you, how they act to you, and how they feel towards you. In doing as such, you free yourself by the weight of conveying another person's conduct on your shoulders. Hence, you do not assimilate other individuals' vitality. It is not all that much.

❖ Find Your Environment

It is not about the external condition. It is mainly about the internal state. It is never where you are at, and it is the place you believe you are at. For what reason is nature so significant? The earth modifies an individual's DNA; however, correctly, it is your recognition that adjusts your DNA. The ground changes your state of mind. How you see yourself oversees what you become. You need to assume 100% liability for where you place yourself. Like never before, when you put yourself in a domain which supplements your vitality, the enchantment begins to occur. What you see with your eyes and what you have within yourself turns into an impression of how you feel. When you encapsulate congruity, you quit engrossing other individuals' vitality, and you begin engraving your energy on your general surroundings.

❖ Let Go of the Need to Be Validated

You need not bother with outer approval. You need support. Commonly along with your life, you look for outside endorsement, which is the reason you begin retaining other individuals' vitality. When you cherish yourself 100%, when you confide in yourself 100%, when you believe in yourself 100%, you start to approve yourself. To quit retaining other individuals' vitality, you need to remain consistent with yourself 100% and enable your legitimacy to thrive and bloom without other individuals' sentiments. Indeed, what others need to state does make a difference, and yet you should wind up mindful of how you respond to other individuals' perspectives. When you begin making a move and stay concentrated on your action; regardless of whether individuals state "frightful" things about you or your work, you are not in any case concerned. Why? Since you cherish what you are doing. The world is about the difference. Differentiation is basic. When you give up to distinction and comprehend that we need grating, you additionally understand that there are continually going to be individuals that will drive you up to the wall, except if you begin changing your point of view and know that these individuals are likewise serving a job on the planet. Remind yourself to associate with the individuals who remind you what your identity is. This encourages you to quit engrossing destructive vitality and to begin retaining progressively positive dynamism.

❖ **The Invitation**

No one can enter your domain without a welcome. You draw in everyone into your life. You are deliberately or unknowingly welcoming individuals into your life, and not consuming other individuals' vitality is to help yourself to remember this every day. You have the power inside to pick whether you need to welcome someone in particular in your sanctuary, which is basically inside yourself.

❖ Do Not Pay Attention

When you get up in the first part of the day, you have so much vitality. For the day you utilize that vitality by offering it to individuals and things around you, until the part of the bargain where it is not much, and you feel tired, and you rest once more. What you need to comprehend is that a few people fill you with vitality and a few people channel you of life. The individuals that direct you of energy are likewise called "vitality vampires." They can be your partners, your companions, or even close relatives. A vitality vampire is somebody who uses your vitality to endure. One of the significant activities is to truly distinguish whether they are transitory vitality vampires or characteristically vitality vampires.

A transitory vitality vampire is somebody who is experiencing a troublesome time in his life or somebody in the family has kicked the bucket, and for a couple of months, they are enthusiastically depleting. Be that as it may, on the off chance that somebody is intrinsically a vitality vampire, at that point, it is incredibly critical to observe that. That is a character attribute that won't change at any point shortly except if they are effectively dealing with it. Most vitality vampires would prefer not to take a shot at themselves at any rate.

Something to do now is to recognize these individuals. One approach to do it, is by asking yourself after you have invested energy with somebody, "Do I feel elevated, or do I feel depleted?" You would prefer not to feel depleted. You need to dodge those individuals. You have buckled down to inspire yourself and be a superior person. For what reason would you permit another person to come and deplete you? There is no motivation to feel regretful about it. Regardless of whether they are a dear companion or a relative, it is alright too, in the end, leave them since what you are doing is taking care of yourself. By elevating yourself, you inspire everybody around you. If you enable someone to pull you down, at that point, you are completing damage to all your different companions and all your other relatives.

By enabling one individual to pull you down, you are not allowing you to inspire the different loved ones that are around you who could be elevated by your quality. When you give somebody consideration, you are giving them vitality. You need to change your concentration to quit retaining other individuals' life. Whatever you center around develops. Is it accurate to say that you are concentrating on what you need, or would you say you are focused on what you dread? You make your existence dependent on considerations and emotions. You need to recall how to shield yourself from hurtful vitality. Make sure to have some good times and grin.

Chapter 12: Empathy and the World

From the news reports and things happening in our neighborhoods, anyone can see that humans are very capable of perpetrating unimaginable cruelty. The vicious nature of human beings knows no bounds; therefore, people result to insulting, bullying, criticizing, torturing, and even killing one another. However, if you ask the perpetrators of this horrible behavior if they would like the same things brought up them, they would say no. And yet, the evil deeds continue to happen every day. The disregard for other people and selfishness seems to be growing.

As conventional healers, empaths can sweep and peruse the vitality of the individuals, places, and articles around them. What's more, as the chakra outline features, the heart chakra is in charge of sentiments of adoration, pardoning, empathy, and confidence. Not at all like the individuals who are overwhelmingly aloof, empaths channel their energies through the heart chakra. They likewise have an unprecedented capacity to effectively direct the majority of the chakras, making them both empathic and mystic, which clarifies why one of the main characteristics of an empath is their inborn capacity to know specific things without being told. The adoration, association, and sympathy empaths radiate are the attributes the world needs increasingly at this moment. Since empaths have elevated affectability and sympathy, they make the best healers and can all the more likely help other people manage the inside feelings or torment they cannot process.

To make matter worse, people continually justify their wrongdoings based on their own small perception of the world without stopping to realize that there could be something wrong with the way they approach life. One of the main causes of the current societal distress is the diminishment of empathy.
In trying times, it is very essential that one considers the feelings of the people around him/her.

Everyone is in their own bubble with unique perspectives on the world, and as such, it is important that every person understands the experiences of the other person. This understanding will help in personal development. Trying to understand the experiences and feelings of the other person is what we have referred to as empathy. Of course, there are those natural reflexes that occur subconsciously without even thinking such as wincing when someone else gets hurt. In order to be truly empathetic, one must actively consider the needs and feelings of other people.

In real life, empathy is one of the essential skills one can apply and practice. Application of empathy in real-life situations will help a person succeed personally and professionally. The more one practices empathy constructively, the higher the levels of happiness. As exhausting as empathy can become for anyone, it has been identified as one of the primary drivers of success and good fortune. Everybody should explicitly work towards enhancing their ability to empathize with other people.

There is a wide variety of reasons why one should practice empathy in real life:

1. With empathy, one is in a better position to treat the people he/she cares about in a better way; more like he/she would want to be treated.
2. Empathy enables one to understand the needs of the people around him/her more clearly.
3. Empathy enables one to understand the perception he/she creates in other people with words and actions.
4. There is a lot of communication done in nonverbal ways. Empathy enables one to understand the non-verbalized parts of communication.
5. In work situations, the person using empathy will understand the customers, work colleagues, and bosses in a better way.
6. Empathy also enhances one's ability to predict and interpret the actions and reactions of people.
7. Once an individual learns how to use empathy, he/she is in a better position to influence and motivate the other people.

8. It will be easier to convince others about a particular viewpoint.
9. Empathy enables one to experience the world on a higher resolution; this is as a result of perceiving the world from a personal angle and the presumptions of other people.
10. Applying empathy in real life also enables one to deal with the negative energies of other people because he/she understands their fears and motives. Empathy enables one to calm down in a difficult situation, and it reminds one to accept things as they are.
11. The overall benefit of applying empathy in real life is that one becomes a better friend, a better follower, and a better leader.

As mentioned earlier, empathy can be a reflex action, but to be empathetic in this world, one must use critical thinking to understand, interpret and offer a solution to the challenges. In order to effectively apply empathy in real life, there are some practices that an empath should use to develop the gift.

Firstly, **Listen.**

Pay a lot of attention when people are speaking to you and to each other. Conversations tend to initiate a back and forth rhythm of speaking, especially when it is about heated topics. One party will start a point even before the other person gets to an end. You will also notice that you are prone to the same habit whereby you already decide what to say next even before the other person has completed his/her point. You feel that your point is too hot and too right to wait. It burns your throat and mind, waiting to be heard.

In conversations, it is important to slow down and wait for the other person to finish even before you can start on your opinion. Force yourself to understand the words you hear without rushing. Do not just consider the conversation and the fact that you want to prove a point; instead, consider the motivation that is behind the words of the speaker. Before jumping to conclusions, consider the experiences that might have forced the person to argue from a particular point of view.

Take time before responding and use visuals and sounds such as 'oh,' 'ah' and 'ya?' to indicate participation. Ask follow-up questions to facilitate a better understanding of the intentions of speakers. Make sure you know their true feelings before responding with a personal opinion. Such conversations will take a longer time because you have to focus on the speaker before you can think of an appropriate answer.

Secondly, **Watch and Wonder.**

In the current world, most of us have developed the habit of staring at the cellphones during every other free minute. While we are waiting for the bus, we are on social media. While we wait for the coffee to be served, we are reading articles online. While we are stuck in the traffic jam, we chat with people who are miles away using the cellphones. Consequently, we miss most of the things taking place around us. It is important that we put the phones and other devices down for a while and observe the people around us. Not that reading the news articles is a bad practice, but it is better if we can also read the faces and expressions of other people. Look at people and try to imagine what they are feeling the things they might be going through, and their next move. This watching and wondering bring about care. You will start feeling for the people around you and applying empathy.

Thirdly, **Know Your Enemies.**
In this context, the word enemy might appear as an exaggeration. However, the application of empathy in real life needs a little more than ordinary. Think of someone with whom you have an ongoing dispute or a tense situation; it can be a coworker who is always criticizing your work and giving you opinions on how it should be done or a family member you are in constant loggerheads with for some reason or the other. Whoever it is, you have already come to the conclusion that they are wrong and you are right. In fact, it gets to a point where you disagree regardless of the topic just because you have to be on opposite sides.

Applying empathy means that you can view the entire situation from the point of view of the other person. Empathy makes one realize that the other person is not selfish or evil. In fact, the person might not be wrong about the things he/she says. In most cases, the problem is more of a basic philosophical difference rather than the specific conflict occurring at the moment.

With empathy, one can understand the following aspects; what causes the other person to feel tenses thus making it hard to reason together? How does the person feel in the event of the disagreement? How does holding the argument exacerbate the fears and tension rather than calming them? What valid opinions does the person make for a particular situation? What are the intentions of the person and are they positive or negative? What is the idea behind the opinions and what motivates it? Is the conflict more important than the idea behind the differing opinions or is the situation worth of compromise?

Once one gathers the answers to these questions, the chances are that the level of anxiety and frustration in life will reduce. In fact, understanding the viewpoints of different people will help one to overcome some of the stressful interpersonal situations. This exercise might sound easy, but it takes practice to make it work.

Choose the Other Side

Empathy can empower a person to be able to see things from the perspective of a third person. Generally, it is hard for a person to take the same side as his/her enemy, and it requires a lot of discipline for one to understand another while thinking about personal emotions and stress. It is important to suspend personal judgment for a while.

Summarily, in order to use empathy effectively in real life, one should consider the following:

1. Put aside personal viewpoints and look at things from other people's perspective. When one does this, he/she realizes that other people are not just being stubborn, unkind, or evil. They just react to issues depending on the knowledge they have.

2. Validate the perspectives of other people. Once you understand why a person is supporting what he/she believes in, acknowledge it. Keep in mind that acknowledgment is not the same as agreeing with a different opinion. It is only accepting that different people have varying opinions for various reasons and they have a good course for holding their opinion.

3. Examine your attitude. Empathy should enable one to check their priorities. Is it more important for you to get

your way, win, or be right? Or do you prefer finding a solution, accepting others, and building relationships? Without an open attitude and mind, you will lack enough room for empathy.

4. Listen – As seen earlier in the topic, it is important to listen to the entire message before giving an opinion. The other person will be communicating both verbally and non-verbally; therefore, listen with your ears, eyes, instincts, and heart. The ears will detect the tone that is being used, the eyes will spot the body language, the instinct will sense when a person is not saying what they mean, and the heart will spot what the other person feels.

5. Ask the other person what he/she would do. When you are in doubt, it is okay to ask the other person about their position. Although most people avoid asking direct questions, it is probably the most effective way of understanding the stand of others. It is okay to ask and remember that figuring it out on your own does not give you extra points. The best part of asking is that you are more likely to get it right. For instance, it would be better if a boss asks the employees what an ideal holiday gift would be rather than giving them all turkey vouchers without checking if they enjoy cooking.

Why Is It Important to Apply Empathy in Real Life?

Without empathy, people would go about their lives without considering the feelings and thoughts of other people. Every person has differing perspectives on life; therefore, if we did not have something that made us accommodate each other, life would be very complicated. We all experience moods, joy, sadness, pain hurt et cetera, and if we focus only on the things happening in our lives, we will limit our capabilities. It is easy to jump into conclusions if we do not take a moment to truly understand what the other people stand for. Lack of empathy normally leads to bad feelings, misunderstandings, poor morale, conflict, and even divorce.

When one uses empathy in real life to understand why a person is angry, or a child is throwing a tantrum, he/she might learn about things in their lives that trigger the behavior. For example, one might find that something happened at home, thus pushing the angry person to act out or that the child did not have a meal in the morning thus they are not okay.

Empathy enables one to ask questions about the situation or behavior of another person before taking a defensive stance or reacting to some emotions. There may still be the need for disciplinary action, but one should use empathy first. Empathy makes a person feel valued and understood even if they are punished for the wrong deeds, and as such, they will accept responsibility for their action. Empathy is currently the missing link in schools, families, workplaces, and the world at large.

There are a few misunderstandings that arise when one is applying empathy in real life. Some people believe that being empathetic involves agreeing with the opinion of everybody else. That is wrong and will only lead to exhaustion. Understand the perceptions of the other person, acknowledge them but you do not have to sing along every tune.

Other people believe that being empathetic involves doing what everyone else wants or doing anything to make others happy. That is wrong. You are not obligated to please everyone; you do not have to cooperate in every other situation. Just because you fail to accommodate every other matter does not mean that you are evil. The world is complicated; therefore, use empathy but do not agree with everything.

Empathy does not mean being there for someone for a lifetime. After listening to a person and offering a solution, you do not have to always be there for them, you have other tasks to accomplish and if you feel that the person is just using you, walk away. Empathy does not mean you should have no ego or intention. Once you assist someone, allow your ego to help you walk away or change the discussion.

Applying empathy in real life can be challenging therefore, there are investments that one needs to make and they include time, patience and proactivity.

1. Time

   It takes some time for one to listen to others, pay attention and not jump into conclusions. Coming up with good solutions also takes time. In most cases, we want to arrive at an answer very first without taking the time to understand; this only leads to more problems. Empathy is like watching sand draining in an hourglass; it takes time, but not that much time, and it is very satisfying.

2. Patience

   Empathy does not only take time; it requires a lot of patience. Paying attention to someone, listening to everything they are saying, and selecting a comprehensive solution takes a lot more than just jumping into conclusions, listing arguments and repeating an opinion. Normally people fail to give the patience and attention required when making conversations; therefore, it becomes harder than it should be.

3. It takes proactivity

   Some people think that empathy should only be given when both parties have something to gain. In the real sense, we should show empathy even to people who show no sign of understanding our perspectives and opinions. This can be very frustrating, and one might find it very unfair, but empathy begins with you. It will not work if both of you wait on each other to start the conversation.

4. Be the role model, set the example, be a good listener and do not talk until the other person is done. Understand the opinions of other people but remember you do not have to agree with them. Being empathetic can be a tough challenge but still, there are many people that practice it. Apply empathy every day and enjoy the benefits.

Conclusion

Thank for making it through to the end of *Empath Survival Guide*, let us hope it was informative and able to provide you with all of the tools you need to achieve your goals whatever they may be.

The next steps will vary from one individual to the next. You may want to do further reading on the science of empathy, or the insights that the field of clinical psychology can offer. Working with a therapist or counselor can be enormously helpful, allowing you to more quickly process and release emotions that haven't originated within you. If you found the chapter on energy healing to be particularly compelling, you might instead choose to schedule a reiki initiation with a master, or look for a school of modern mysteries to provide further guidance on advanced spiritual practice. It is important for empaths with any degree of power to continually monitor their emotional balance, purge negativity, replenish energy, and seek higher clarity and truth. Embrace these practices as part of a lifelong journey and recognize that even if you ascend to the level of a spiritual teacher or guide for others, there will always be more to learn.

No matter how empowered one may become, and regardless of how well one has honed their empathic power, it is important to embrace humility, keep the mind open to unexpected possibilities. The self-righteous empath who develops a hermetic view of the world, unwilling to entertain ideas that do not strongly resonate with their interior knowledge, is likely to be deeply discontented or anxious, and struggle with communication and loving relationships, as others will perceive them to be arrogant and standoffish.

This type of attitude is also likely to weaken your empathic powers. Truth is multifaceted and always changing. In order to grasp even a sliver of it, the empath must maintain a balanced connection between their interior and exterior worlds. Shutting either out, or favoring one over the other, will eventually lead the empath to receive misleading messages, or lead them to misinterpret messages that would otherwise be clear and easy to decipher. Empaths are privy to knowledge that often goes unseen, unheard, unacknowledged, but from time to time, they can be flat out wrong--especially if the information they're receiving from the exterior world is limited, it can be skewed to support an incomplete hypothesis.

It can also be incredibly healing and inspiring to open your eyes to all the empathic power around you, much of which is still dormant, not yet fully realized or understood. Use the metrics outlined in the second and third chapter of this book and ask yourself if you might know other empaths who haven't awakened their sensitive powers. Or perhaps you know some self-aware empaths that you couldn't recognize as such before now. Whatever the case, you can benefit immensely from expanding your empathic support system. Since empaths are often able to see everything clearly except them; let your fellow empaths be a metaphysical mirror. Teach each other, trust each other; heal each other, replenish and amplify each other's energies. You may discover an echelon of both outward love and self-love that you never knew existed before.

Finally, if you found this book beneficial in any way, a review on Amazon is always welcome!

CPSIA information can be obtained
at www.ICGtesting.com
Printed in the USA
BVHW090828220221
600777BV00001B/52